CROSSCURRENTS *Modern Critiques*

CROSSCURRENTS *Modern Critiques*
Harry T. Moore, *General Editor*

William McMurray

THE LITERARY REALISM
OF William Dean Howells

WITH A PREFACE BY
Harry T. Moore

Carbondale and Edwardsville

SOUTHERN ILLINOIS UNIVERSITY PRESS

FEFFER & SIMONS, INC.

London and Amsterdam

PREFACE

WILLIAM MC MURRAY *stresses the realism of William Dean Howells, which is the principal characteristic of his writings. Mr. McMurray calls attention to this throughout his excellent examination of Howells' principal novels, each of them considered as a unit and yet as a unit related to a general pattern. This book suggests that Howells' approach to realism was both a philosophy of life and a discipline.*

It has been pleasant for many of us, in the last decade or so, to observe how well Howells has held his reputation, even increased it. As for writing anything extensive about him, at present, however, I find myself unable to go beyond what I said, in a highly concentrated form, in my Afterword to the Signet Classics edition of The Rise of Silas Lapham. There, besides discussing that particular story, I deal with various phases of Howells, including his move from what was virtually a frontier to the great cities of Boston and New York—oddly enough, by way of Venice. In that essay I also point out Howells' relation to—really his difference from—such authors as Theodore Dreiser and Sinclair Lewis, while also indicating how Silas Lapham embodies the capitalism-cum-religion theories of Max Weber and R. H. Tawney. The latter observation applies not only to Lapham but to other

Howells characters of the business-as-sacrament type, such as Conrad Dryfoos in A Hazard of New Fortunes.

I had the pleasure of discussing that novel, in 1957, on one of several appearances on the CBS program, "Invitation to Learning," now alas no longer being broadcast. On the program devoted to A Hazard of New Fortunes, Alfred Kazin and I were the guests of Lyman Bryson. I've just replayed the recording of that and find Alfred Kazin using a wonderful phrase, growing out of Howells' years as a printer's devil, to the effect that "he wrote like a man who had learned English at the fountainhead of print."

That applies, wonderfully, as do Mr. McMurray's investigations of Howells' use of realism as a mode of the understanding of life. Mr. McMurray's book is a young man's book with many allusions to the discoveries of his predecessors. They have a somewhat anthological value without greatly diminishing the original outlook of Mr. McMurray himself, who in future volumes will perhaps rely somewhat more on the strength of his own vision and judgment. Meanwhile he has given us an excellent study of William Dean Howells, incisive and valuable, for which we should be grateful.

HARRY T. MOORE

Southern Illinois University
November 11, 1966

CONTENTS

MY PURPOSE in this study of twelve of William Dean Howells' novels, from the early *A Foregone Conclusion* (1875) to *The Vacation of the Kelwyns* (1920), published in the year of the novelist's death, is to offer readings of them. What the readings reveal, I find, is a similarity of conceptual pattern which defines a basic attitude of the writer toward life. This basic attitude, I suggest, and as was first suggested to me by Professor George Arms, has remarkably much in common with the pragmatism of William James, who was contemporary with Howells.

If my thesis then is that Howells' literary realism closely resembles James's pragmatism, I, nonetheless, would like to think that the readings of the novels are valuable in themselves for what they show as readings. Taken as a whole, the readings may seem repetitious. Yet, it is interesting to see how the individual novels establish their different subjects within a unity of pattern. At the same time the book may be read in its parts, for each reading of a novel is complete in itself.

My reading of the novels has convinced me that Howells was a much more self-aware and skillful novelist than is generally assumed, and to recognize the resemblance between his realism and James's pragmatism is not only to sharpen one's sense of the dimensions of Howells' realism, it also heightens one's awareness of the intellectual America that Howells and James shared in common. In this sense, then, the readings offered here may be regarded as an introduction both to Howells' realism and to the world in which the novelist lived.

I want to thank Duke University Press and *The New England Quarterly* for permission to use revised articles which appeared as "Point of View in Howells' *The Landlord at Lion's Head*" (*American Literature*, May, 1962) and "The Concept of Complicity in Howells' Fiction" (*The New England Quarterly*, December, 1962) and to acknowledge a first appearance of my chapters on *A Modern Instance* in *Research and Studies*, Madison College, Virginia.

WILLIAM MC MURRAY

Madison College
Harrisonburg, Virginia
October 1965

THE LITERARY REALISM
OF William Dean Howells

PUBLISHED in 1875, A *Foregone Conclusion* is one of
Howells' earliest fictions written in that realistic mode
which he would employ throughout his long career.
Set in Venice, the story centers on Don Ippolito, an
Italian priest who is unable to believe in his priesthood and who dreams of escaping from it to live as a
man. Sharing in the priest's story are Henry Ferris,
acting officially as American Consul but who thinks of
himself as really a painter; Florida Vervain, a lovely
and ardent American girl; and Mrs. Vervain, Florida's
flighty but well-meaning mother. How Don Ippolito
falls in love with Florida, who has promised to help
him to freedom in America, and how Florida rejects
the priest and ultimately is wedded with Ferris is the
substance of the story. The problem of the novel is to
understand Don Ippolito's situation. It suggests that
the full freedom in an uncomplex and unified identity
which he seeks can never be realized because of the
continuing conflict between the inner life of intention
and spirit and the outer one of actuality. Don Ippolito
is able to reconcile his conflict only by accepting the
imperfection of his human situation.

As the story opens, Don Ippolito has approached
the American Consul, Ferris, with a request for a
passport to America. Don Ippolito carries with him a

cannon he has invented, which he imagines would be useful to the Union forces in the American Civil War. Because Don Ippolito is not an American, however. Ferris cannot issue him a passport: "You know . . . no government can give passports to foreign subjects. That would be an unheard of thing." [1] Olov W. Fryckstedt observes that in Don Ippolito's Venice "barriers" were everywhere—"political, spiritual. social, and economic; they all tended to curb and frustrate the ambitions and the hopes of the individual. . . . Naturally, a product of such a society would be entirely different from people who had grown up and lived in America." [2] In his complex situation, with "barriers" everywhere, Don Ippolito dreams of going to America, "to that new world of freedom and justice" (p. 254), he tells Florida. The degree and nature of Don Ippolito's complex situation are detailed in the scene with Ferris. An Italian priest living in Venice, Don Ippolito is an Austrian subject. Although his native language is Italian, Don Ippolito also speaks a broken English with "a fine brogue superimposed upon his Italian accent" that puzzles Ferris until Don Ippolito explains that he had studied the language with an English ecclesiastic from Dublin who had been visiting in Venice. Barriers, indeed, are the actualities of man's condition everywhere; and if America, as the land of freedom and justice, seems to Don Ippolito to promise escape from barriers, it is because he does not understand the significance of the American Civil War to which he would contribute his invented cannon. Don Ippolito explains to Ferris that the cannon is designed with a hidden chamber containing explosive material. Should an enemy seize the weapon, Don Ippolito continues, the hidden explosive would go off and kill him. Ferris objects that the cannon is impractical. Suppose, he says, that from the heat of constant firing at the enemy, the hidden explosive went off and killed the person operating the cannon? In the cannon, Howells subtly hints at Don Ippolito's own conflict between his hidden self and his outward one as a priest. By extension, the cannon stands for man's existence as a kind of perpetual war between self and others, a situation ever present in a world of "barriers." In whatever terms man's war in his dual existence may be conceived, it is clear that there is no safe "side": a weapon meant to kill the enemy may kill one's self.

Through Ferris, Don Ippolito is engaged as Italian teacher for Florida Vervain. Mrs. Vervain has felt that her daughter should be tutored while they are living in Europe; but in the past Florida's tutors have always fallen in love with her, a fact which has been embarrassing and even offensive to Florida's innocence. Not without some skepticism, Ferris suggests to Mrs. Vervain that Don Ippolito will perhaps solve the tutor problem; for, as a priest, he is " 'professionally pledged . . . not to give the kind of annoyance you've suffered from in teachers.' "

In his new role as Florida's teacher, Don Ippolito expands in the freedom of his relationship with the Vervains. As he later tells Florida, " 'You have been willing to see the man in me, and to let me forget the priest' " (p. 167). Appearing one day at the Vervains' in a new costume, Don Ippolito is considerably altered in appearance. Having shed his priestly habit, he now wears new stockings, hat, and coat—all giving a decidedly "worldly" air. "The stockings were indeed new, and the hat was not the accustomed *nicchio*, but a new silk cylinder with a very worldly, curling brim. Don Ippolito's coat, also, was of a more mundane cut than the *talare*; he wore a waistcoat and smallclothes, meeting the stockings at the knee with a sprightly

buckle." Mrs. Vervain gives a start and, "adjusting her
glasses," says: " 'I shouldn't have known you!' " It is
becoming, Mrs. Vervain observes, " 'but it does look
so out of character. . . . It's like seeing a military
man in a civil coat' " (p. 95). Florida, recalling that
her father, Colonel Vervain, used sometimes to leave
off his uniform, remarks: It must " 'be a great relief to
lay aside the uniform now and then.' " Smiling pain-
fully, Don Ippolito confusedly blunders into a story
about how he and a friend, when in subdeaconate
orders, once left off their priestly dress during a week-
end in Padua. His story is received in stunned silence, "as if something shocking had been said." On
the next day, says the narrator, "the priest came in his
usual dress, and he did not again try to escape from it"
(p. 97).

Nevertheless, Don Ippolito does not give up his
dream of escaping from his priesthood. Eventually, he
tells Florida of his ambition to go to America where,
as an inventor, he will live as other men do. All his life
as a priest, says Don Ippolito, has been a lie; while
Florida, he tells her, has all her life lived the truth.

> ". . . you have the life-long habit of the truth. Do you
> know what it is to have the life-long habit of a lie? It is
> to be a priest. Do you know what it is to seem, to say, to
> do, the thing you are not, think not, will not? To leave
> what you believe unspoken, what you will undone, what
> you are unknown? It is to be a priest!" (p. 168)

Her heart going out to the poor priest whose life is a
lie, a mere appearance of truth, Florida asks him
whether he believes in his Church. " 'I have no
Church,' " he replies. Surely, though, he believes in
God? " 'I do not know,' " Don Ippolito whispers.

The problem of truth and belief is pervasive in all
of Howells' fiction. In *A Foregone Conclusion*

Howells, writes Fryckstedt, "also wanted to use as a theme what he considered another major difference between Italians and Americans: their totally divergent attitudes towards truth. Ferris expressed Howells' views when he said about the Italians that they 'are a kinder people than we are, but they're not so just, and I should say that they didn't think truth the chief good of life.' " [3] Delmar Gross Cooke noted Don Ippolito's "double life" as well as Florida's "devotion to the truth." [4] More recently, George N. Bennett has said: "The truth about Don Ippolito, Howells was being careful to say, like most truths, can only be stated as an approximation. It lies somewhere among the views produced by Florida's sympathetic innocence, Ferris's compassionate but not disinterested scepticism, and Mrs. Vervain's well-intentioned but unperceptive superficiality." [5] Finally, Edwin H. Cady speaks of everything in Howells' novel as converging in "the tragic moment when the full folly of the illusions in which all the characters have been moving, each bemused by his own, is revealed." [6] Anticipating the pragmatism of William James, Howells repeatedly demonstrated in his fiction that truth is relative rather than absolute in experience and that it was emergent in that experience. Truth grew out of the facts, and what the facts meant was known in their consequences for experience. For Howells the truth about Don Ippolito had to begin somewhere to show itself, and it began this showing of itself in the facts—limited and imperfect as that truth was. The attitude of the realist was pragmatic, and the pragmatic attitude, James said, meant "looking away from first things, principles, 'categories,' supposed necessities; and of looking towards last things, fruits, consequences, facts." [7] Emergent in experience, truth was not fixed and static nor given. Truth changed as man made shift to adapt his "old" self—with all its aspirations, hopes, beliefs—to changing actualities in the world around him. At once psychological and metaphysical in its dimensions, man's truth, Howells saw, was forever incomplete and unfinished in the forms it took in man's continuing quest for ultimate truth, for absolute knowledge.

One scene in A *Foregone Conclusion* humorously juxtaposes man's conception of an ideal truth with actuality. Significantly, it is the celebration of Corpus Christi, and Florida and Ferris have gone to see Don Ippolito march in one of the processions. Howells paints the scene in all the color of its pagentry, but as we view it through the eyes of Florida and Ferris we are struck by the ludicrous incongruity of the whole where human persons are costumed as heavenly beings. A motley, it makes Florida sad. She questions whether " 'it might all be a mistake after all; perhaps there might not be any other world, and every bit of this power and display of the church—*our* church as well as the rest—might be only a cruel blunder, a dreadful mistake. Perhaps there isn't even any God!' " Ferris, looking at a troop of soldiers marching in front of a procession representing "the followers of the Lamb," skeptically cries out: " 'Great God! How far it is from Christ! Look there, at those troops who go before the followers of the Lamb: their trade is murder' " (p. 202). From the opening pages of the novel, Howells has prepared us for the full weight of Ferris' remark: Don Ippolito's personal conflict, symbolized in his cannon, is the equation for that dilemma of the world which Ferris sees in the Corpus Christi procession. In brief, the conflict is between the human dream of an ideal truth and the human actuality. Watching the faces of the priests in the procession, Florida exclaims that they all " 'look false and sly and

bad—*all* of them!' " Ferris, though, declares that
" 'good, kind, friendly faces' " are in the majority;
and, singling one out, says: " 'There . . . that's what
I call an uncommonly good face.' " At that moment
the face looks directly up to the balcony over the
street where Ferris stands with Florida. " 'Why,' said
Ferris aloud, 'it's Don Ippolito!' " (p. 205).

Howells shows truth as relative and impressionistic
in his novel by linking truth with art, thereby suggesting an affinity between moral and aesthetic knowledge. Ferris has begun a portrait of Don Ippolito. An
"uncompromising enemy of the theatricalisation of
Italy, or indeed of anything," says the narrator, Ferris
aims to paint the real man behind the surface trap-
pings of the Venetian priest. What he intends, Ferris
tells Florida is

". . . to paint *at* . . . the lingering pagan in the man,
the renunciation first of the inherited nature, and then
of a personality that would have enjoyed the world. I
want to show that baffled aspiration, apathetic despair,
and rebellious longing which you catch in his face when
he's off his guard, and that suppressed look which is the
characteristic expression of all Austrian Venice. Then
. . . I must work in that small suspicion of Jesuit there
is in every priest." (p. 92)

Florida, from her own single-minded and innocent
view, tells Ferris that if he puts " 'all that' " into the
picture it won't be Don Ippolito at all. " 'He has the
simplest and openest look in the world,' " she says.
Ferris later complains to Don Ippolito that the portrait is proving troublesome. " 'There are too many of
you,' " he tells Don Ippolito. Looking at the unfinished portrait of himself, Don Ippolito remarks: " 'I
suppose that it resembles me a great deal . . . and
yet I do not *feel* like that.' " Then, in unconscious
irony, he adds: " 'I hardly know what is the fault. It is

as I should be if I were like other priests, perhaps?' "
Admitting that it " '*is* conventional, in spite of everything,' " Ferris brings out the first sketch he had done
of Don Ippolito. It "was vastly sincerer and sweeter"
and is to Don Ippolito's immediate liking. Seeing this
picture of himself, Don Ippolito is suddenly moved to
reveal to Ferris his love for Florida. Shocked, Ferris
exclaims: " 'You? You! A priest?' " Angered and hurt,
Don Ippolito breaks out into an impassioned declaration of freedom, boasting that he can offer to Florida
" 'the honourable love of a man—the truth of a most
sacred marriage, and fidelity to death!' " Pleading then
for justice, Don Ippolito asks for recognition of his
manhood, and though he speaks in the role of the
priest, Howells lets us hear Shakespeare's Jew, too.

> "And at heart, what is a priest, then, but a man?—a
> wretched, masked, imprisoned, banished man! Has he
> not blood and nerves like you? Has he not eyes to see
> what is fair, and ears to hear what is sweet? Can he live
> near so divine a flower and not know her grace, not
> inhale the fragrance of her soul, not adore her beauty?
> Oh, great God! And if at last he would tear off his
> stifling mask, escape from his prison, return from his
> exile, would you gainsay him?" (pp. 230–31)

Ferris urges Don Ippolito to consider that perhaps
Florida does not return his love, that her feeling may
be only an excessive atonement for having once been
sharp with Don Ippolito when the priest innocently
remarked on Florida's devotion to her mother. It may
be, continues Ferris, that Florida is " 'only trying to
appeal to something in you as high as the impulse of
her own heart.' " Don Ippolito asks: " 'Can there be
any higher thing in heaven or on earth than love for
such a woman?' " " 'Yes,' " answers Ferris, " 'both in
heaven and on earth.' " Here, Ferris appeals to a
higher love than that of man for woman—love of

God. But the priest speaks for the love between man and woman. The reversal of roles between priest and man is ironic. If Ferris aimed at painting the lingering pagan in the priest, he now disavows that aim when his idea of Don Ippolito is put to the test. The distinction between moral and aesthetic truth made by Ferris, however, is not made by Howells. The truth for Howells, rather, is problematic; and distinctions between moral and aesthetic knowledge, for the realist, are relative.

The moment in the novel in which, as Cady has suggested, the illusions of the characters are revealed and which Henry James called its "finest," is the one in the moonlit Venetian garden where Don Ippolito at last confesses to Florida his love. Elated by his talk with Florida about their proposed journey to America and the new life he will live there, Don Ippolito is moved to turn on a fountain in the garden—though Florida scrupulously warns that they must not waste the water. Don Ippolito tells her that he only wants to " 'let it play a moment.' " As he watches the fountain in the moonlight, Don Ippolito feels himself free. For the moment he seems to find a kind of absolute repose in the whiteness of the moonlit sky, a whiteness that is reflected by the flowers in the darkness of the garden that merges with the blackness of the priest's garment. The picture, with its fertile ambiguity of light and dark, is the truest portrait of Don Ippolito in the novel.

> The moon painted his lifted face with a pallor that his black robes heightened. He fetched a long, sighing breath, as if he inhaled with that respiration all the rich odours of the flowers, blanched like his own visage in the white lustre; as if he absorbed into his heart at once the wide glory of the summer night, and the beauty of the young girl at his side. It seemed a supreme moment

with him; he looked as a man might look who has climbed out of life-long defeat into a single instant of release and triumph. (p. 251)

Here, in the shadowed light of a reality that is more like a dream, Howells paints his priest-man in his elusive truth and identity. The scene is Hawthornian —not only in depiction, but in idea as well; for, like Hawthorne, Howells well knew how "real" life is itself a romance. Nor does Howells here give full weight to the tragic implications in this illusion of reality in the garden. Delicately he undermines Don Ippolito's momentary "triumph": "Florida sank upon the bench before the fountain indulging his caprice with that sacred, motherly tolerance, some touch of which is in all womanly yielding to men's will, and which was perhaps present in greater degree in her feeling towards a man more than ordinarily orphaned and unfriended" (pp. 251–52). A man "more than ordinarily orphaned and unfriended," Florida thinks the priest; and, thinking it, feels for him, a "sacred, motherly tolerance." With a careful irony, shading tragedy into compassionate comedy, Howells skillfully hints at the mysterious complicity of all life, a complicity that is at once a union and an alienation of man in the world. Confessing to Florida that he loves her, Don Ippolito hears her exclaim: " 'You? A priest!' " He then cries out, in a shock of recognition: " 'It is true, I cannot escape, I am doomed, I must die as I have lived!' " (p. 255). Overcome by her sympathy for the priest, Florida reaches out and kisses his head. Unknown to them both, Ferris has unintentionally witnessed the last of the scene from behind a tree. He believes that Florida and Don Ippolito have sealed their love.

Following the departure of Mrs. Vervain and Florida from Venice, Don Ippolito is taken ill with a fever. He calls Ferris to his bedside to tell him that he has found peace at last in accepting his priesthood, as Florida had once suggested he might do. " 'I have found peace where she bade me seek it . . . I have mastered my affliction by reconciling myself to it,' " he says, asking Ferris to tell this to Florida (p. 285). Ferris can only believe the priest is lying. The whole thing strikes him as being too much like a conventional death-bed conversion and affects him "as unreally as talk in a stage-play." Don Ippolito finally tells Ferris that it was "*you*" Florida loved. Before Ferris can see Don Ippolito again, word is brought to him that the priest is dead.

Reviewing Howells' novel for *The Nation* in 1875, Henry James expressed dissatisfaction with "the felicity of the episodes related in the last twenty pages of the tale." [8] For James, the novel really ended "when the hero dies." Critical comment since James has ignored or tended to scant the concluding section of the novel. Indeed, Howells himself said that, had it not been for publication exigencies, "the story would have ended with Don Ippolito's rejection." [9] George N. Bennett, however, argues that "One effect of the continuation" of the novel "is to modify the tragic emphasis produced by the climactic scene of Don Ippolito's rejection. That scene must be read in a total context, and part of the context is the deliberate reduction from tragic proportions to a life-size 'tragicocomic end of the whole business.' " [10] Bennett's is a good point. The "tragico-comic end of the whole business" is Ferris' remark near the end of the novel when he is thinking of hanging his portrait of Don Ippolito in a New York exhibition in hopes of raising some money by its sale. "He was thinking in a thoroughly vanquished mood what a tragico-comic end of the whole business it was that poor Don Ippolito should come to his rescue in this fashion, and as it were to succour him in his extremity" (p. 297). Having left Venice two years ago after the death of Don Ippolito, Ferris since then has carried in his heart his love for Florida—who had remained in Europe until her mother's death—and has fought and been wounded in the American Civil War on the side of the Union forces. Early in the novel we saw that Don Ippolito, a man at war with himself, had ineffectually offered his services for the Union cause. Now at last, just before he learns from Florida that she loves him and just before their union in marriage, Ferris has been wounded in civil war for the Union cause. The point is that Howells caps the war-peace motif—man's division and union—in the marriage of Florida and Ferris. In the eventual meeting of Ferris and Florida in a New York art museum and in their recognition of their love before the portrait of Don Ippolito, Howells hints at a reconciliation of those conflicting truths and points of view which are thematically central in his novel. Florida, asking Ferris not to sell his portrait of Don Ippolito, says: " 'He did bring us together, after all' " (p. 310). Though symbolic reconciliation is effective in the love and marriage of Florida and Ferris, there still remains a final ambiguity of dark and light in the ultimate meaning of Don Ippolito; for, though united in marriage, Ferris and Florida keep different views toward the priest. Thus, says Howells man's conflict in union, dramatized in the lonely struggle of Don Ippolito to unite his priesthood and his manhood, to make the actual and the ideal one, is his passion in the enduring mystery of painful earth. Failing to grasp the full significance of Don Ippolito, Ferris, in the end, can find only that the priest's life was a "puzzle." The last words, though, are the narrator's.

Thus lapsing more and more into a mere problem as the years have passed, Don Ippolito has at last ceased to be even the memory of a man with a passionate love and a mortal sorrow. Perhaps this final effect in the mind of him who has realised the happiness of which the poor priest vainly dreamed is not the least tragic phase of the tragedy of Don Ippolito.

If Howells' strategy in the concluding portion of his story seems less than satisfactory as art, it is nonetheless true to his conception of the novel and vindicates his own belief that he had "deepened the shadows by going on, and achieved a completer verity, also." [11]

2   THE LADY OF THE
AROOSTOOK

LYDIA BLOOD, a young and lovely girl from South Bradfield, Massachusetts, is the "lady" in Howells' *The
Lady of the Aroostook,* a realist's comedy of manners.
In the story, Lydia sails to Europe on the *Aroostook,* a
ship manned by a "Down East" crew under a fatherly
Captain Jenness. Other passengers are three young
men from Boston. Two of them, Staniford and Dunham, are quite proper; and Staniford will at the last
love and marry Lydia. Hicks, the third male passenger,
is a not-so-proper Bostonian who has been sent to sea
to take the cure. His periodic drunkenness serves in
the novel to comment on the vagaries of morality.
Since Lydia is the only woman on the ship, the story
deals with the uniqueness of this situation and what
the American men make of it. Not until her arrival in
Venice does Lydia see her voyage aboard the good
ship *Aroostook* in a different and darker light; and it is
within this larger framework of contrasting views of
morals and manners that Howells would have us see
his lady.

In South Bradfield, Lydia lives with her aunt, Miss
Maria Latham, and with her mother's father—decent
New England folks. Miss Maria, "an elderly woman
with a plain, honest face," surveys the world from her
favorite "haircloth arm-chair." Both she and Lydia's

grandfather are apprehensive about Lydia's leaving home, though they accept it for her good. Grandfather reasons: " 'I presume her gifts were given her for improvement, and it would be the same as buryin' them in the ground for her to stay up here.' " [1] What Lydia's gifts are is not made clear. Later, we learn that she has a "peculiarly rich and flexible" singing voice, inherited from her mother. Presumably, then, Lydia is off to Europe to study music. Actually, however, she falls in love with Stainford, and her voyage ends in marriage.

Aboard the *Aroostook* Captain Jenness urges Lydia to make herself at home—in a cabin fitted out for his wife and daughters when they travel with him. Proudly showing Lydia his ship, Captain Jenness boasts: " 'Yes, Miss Blood . . . one difference between an American ship and any other is dirt.' " Captain Jenness speaks truly: the deck of the *Aroostook*, Lydia observes, is "as clean scrubbed as her aunt's kitchen floor." The *Aroostook*, says the Captain to Lydia, " 'is yours as long as you stay in her.' "

Having established the idea of the "purity" of the American ship, Lydia's ship, Howells begins exploring it. With the help of Thomas, a boy steward, Lydia settles into her cabin. Its "snugness of . . . arrangement" brings "a light of housewifely joy" to Lydia's face. Thomas asks her to call him by his name rather than by title, explaining: " 'They said you'd call me steward . . . and as long as I've not got my growth, it kind of makes them laugh. . . .' " Unpacking, Lydia herself laughs. Thomas, blushing, asks what she is laughing at. Nothing, Lydia replies, only: " 'My aunt told me if any of these things should happen to want doing up, I had better get the stewardess to help me.' " As Lydia unpacks a "black silk dress," Thomas' eyes widen, and he asks whether Lydia is going to wear it on the ship. Pleased, Lydia answers: " 'Sundays, perhaps' " (p. 30). With the black dress a faint shadow falls over the immaculate, white-sailed *Aroostook*. Later, visiting the galley with Dunham, whose devotion to the sacredness of womankind has prompted him to be of all possible service to Lydia, she exclaims at finding a male Negro as the cook. " 'I thought the cook was a woman!' " says Lydia. Clearly, Lydia's preconceptions do not fit the facts: neither the steward nor the cook is a woman. When word gets back to Miss Maria that Lydia is the only woman on the *Aroostook*, she wonders "who in Time . . . will she go to, then?" In time, of course, Lydia will go to Staniford! The first morning out in the ship on which Captain Jenness has urged Lydia to be at home, she wakens after a night of homesickness: "she thought she heard the crowing of a cock and the cackle of hens, and fancied herself in her room at home" (p. 39). The "home" motif extends throughout the novel with the concept of home changing and expanding to embrace a complexity of significance. An instance of it, associated again with birds, is Dunham's pointing out in the galley some hens and roosters, "devoted birds." As Dunham takes a "cockerel" from its cage to show it to Lydia, the bird flies from his hand out over the sea and, says the narrator, is a "suicide."

A "very sincere person" to whom women are "dear and sacred," Dunham does his best to make Lydia feel at home in her peculiar situation. Both he and Staniford, who assumes a critical attitude toward Lydia's country innocence, agree that they must keep Lydia from feeling there is anything "irregular" in her presence on the ship. Staniford is uneasy though and wishes Captain Jenness had warned him there was to be a woman along. He supposes that Jenness " 'thought that if *she* could stand it, *we* might. There's that point of view.' " Staniford becomes increasingly interested in Lydia, deciding that she is clearly a case of " 'supernatural innocence' " (p. 57). He doubts that Lydia finds anything anomalous in her situation and fancies that he and Dunham will be able to keep her " 'unconsciousness intact.' "

Talking over his plans for the future with Staniford, Dunham reveals that he is on his way to Dresden to meet and marry a "divine" Miss Hibbard. Staniford, on the other hand, seems to have no fixed plans. Having tried his hand at the arts—painting, sculpture, writing—he remains dissatisfied. " 'I have,' " he tells Dunham, " 'the noble earth-hunger; I must get upon the land.' " And he dreams of a cattle ranch or sheep range somewhere in the West, perhaps California. When Dunham urges that he should not go West without a wife, Staniford quips, " 'What nice girl would go?' " Some "savage woman," Staniford muses, must rear his "dusky race." Staniford then reflects that Lydia is not one of your "fair" Yankees. " 'There must have been,' " he continues, " 'a good many dark Puritans. In fact, we always think of Puritans as dark, don't we?' " Dunham's reply recalls to us Lydia's black silk dress for Sundays: " 'I believe we do. . . . Perhaps on account of their black clothes' " (p. 68). The shadow over the *Aroostook* and Lydia Blood deepens. Already, it seems, Venice and the "wicked Old World" loom on the horizon of Lydia's maiden voyage. Increasingly, in subtle cross-reference, the certainty of Lydia's meaning gives way to ambiguity. A daughter of the New England Puritans, Lydia is nonetheless a dark-haired beauty who becomes, in the context of Staniford's conversation, a "savage" to mother his "dusky race." From the cross-reference, then, emerges the image of a mixed reality in Lydia Blood that is a foreshadowing of the conflicting views of her once she reaches the Old World of Europe.

Meanwhile, aboard the *Aroostook*, Lydia, "picturesquely," says the narrator, is "the centre about which the ship's pride and chivalrous sentiment" revolves. "They were Americans, and they knew how to worship a woman" (p. 95). Passive and gentle, Lydia beguiles the imagination of Staniford. "He was one of those men who cannot rest in regard to people they meet till they have made some effort to formulate them. He liked to ticket them off. . . ." (p. 90). Lydia seems to him, though, to elude all his formulas, and he comes to feel "more than ever that he must protect this helpless loveliness, since it had begun to please his imagination."

Of importance in Stainford's developing relationship with Lydia is his discovery of her beautiful singing voice. On the Sunday morning when she sings at the religious service, Lydia appears in her black silk dress. "She came out to breakfast in it, and it swept the narrow spaces, as she emerged from her stateroom, with so rich and deep a murmur that every one looked up." The rich and deep murmur of Lydia is not simply a hint of her sexuality; rather, it is a promise of that fertility of significance and meaning which she realizes for us in the whole of the novel. It is a promise of the richness of her impure reality. At Sunday service Lydia, says the narrator, "sang as she did in the meeting-house at South Bradfield, and her voice seemed to fill the hollow height and distance; it rang far off like a mermaid's singing, on high like an angel's; it called with the same deep appeal to sense and soul alike. The sailors stood rapt . . . " (p. 113). Lydia's is the voice of creation, containing in its music, Howells seems to say, the harmony of all the spheres. The service concluded, Staniford says to Dunham:

"Really, that voice puts a new complexion on Miss Blood. I have a theory to reconstruct. I have been philosophizing her as a simple country girl. I must begin on an operatic novice. I liked the other one better. It gave value to the black silk; as a singer she'll wear silk as habitually as a cocoon. She will have to take some stage name; translate Blood into La Sanguinelli. . . . I don't know; I think I preferred the idyllic flavor I was beginning to find in the presence of the ordinary, futureless young girl, voyaging under the chaperonage of her own innocence,—the Little Sister of the Whole Ship." (pp. 114–15)

Dunham, who has a passion for organizing things, gets up a musicale to pass the time, and he asks Hicks to join in. While he does not sing, Hicks, facetiously, says he can play the flute. Hicks has an air "at once amiable and baddish, with an expression, curiously blended, of monkey-like humor and spaniel-like apprehensiveness." Staniford dislikes him, and is "disappointed not to find" Hicks's feet "cloven." Living something of a double life in going from drunkenness to sobriety, Hicks is an outlaw on board the proper *Aroostook*. Following up Hicks's remark that he can play the flute, Staniford suggests a "sacred" concert with Hicks representing "the shawns and cymbals with his flute." Captain Jenness objects that it seems a "kind of blasphemy" to jest about "these scriptural instruments." Hicks says that he did not think of the day as being Sunday, though—"or any more Sunday than usual; seems as if we had had a month of Sundays already since we sailed. I'm not much on religion myself, but I shouldn't like to interfere with other people's principles." The talk turns then to customs of religious practice and observance. At South Bradfield, for instance, it used to be that the Sabbath ended at sundown on Sunday evening. Captain Jenness interjects that Saturday night was kept, too, down in Maine. He says: " 'It came pretty hard to begin so soon, but it seemed to kind of break it, after all, having a night in.' " Staniford, in a remark that puzzles the Captain, laughingly says: " 'Our Puritan ancestors knew just how much human nature could stand, after all. We did not have uninterrupted Sabbath till the Sabbath had become much milder. Is that it?' " (p. 118)

As with "Sunday," so with Lydia. The meaning of both is complex in actual experience. When Mrs. Dunham says near the end of the novel that Lydia " 'was simply a country girl . . . there was *nothing* to her' " (p. 320), she is both right and wrong. Lydia may be a simple country girl, but there is a great deal to her. There is that supreme innocence which the Americans see, and there is that shameful guilt the Europeans find. When both these views focus on Lydia, who is associated in the novel with religion and sex, the full range of Howells' ambiguity asserts itself. Rather than one thing, Lydia means different things. Though she never explicitly understands herself in this way, she nevertheless, is aware at the last of the difference of views toward her and is then better able to live more freely and richly than before—as her marriage with Staniford suggests. Lydia, Staniford remarks, " 'is a deep one.' " She is indeed deep if we look into her for some ultimate and final reality. She is all surface, though, if her reality is only made up of manners. Howells, in the end, does not say which she is—deep or shallow. Rather, she is what she is in her experience. Staniford's good fortune is that he cannot "formulate" Lydia. As he realizes this inability, his generosity, educated when he rescues Hicks from the ocean, grows until as George N. Bennett has observed, Staniford gradually sheds his prejudices and is able to accept Lydia "on her own terms." [2] Staniford no longer insists on restricting Lydia to any conventional view of her. He gives up trying to make her fit into his formulations of who and what she is. This is not only freedom for himself, it also helps Lydia to accept his love.

Near the close of the novel, in Venice now with Staniford and Lydia married, Staniford tells Captain Jenness that " 'if it hadn't been for Hicks perhaps I mightn't have been here.' " For Hicks proves instrumental in bringing Lydia and Staniford together. Staniford notices, for example, that Hicks is able to make Lydia, usually so demure, laugh "freely" and "heartily." Unconsciously, Lydia responds to the unstable Hicks, sensing in him perhaps a lawlessness that complements her own conventional morality. In his struggle to control his own life, Hicks is aware, as Lydia is not, of the precariousness of goodness in the face of disruptive forces in the human personality. When Hicks gives out and gets drunk, however, Lydia has no sympathy for him. She, says the narrator, "had never relented in her abhorrence of Hicks since the day of his disgrace There seemed no scorn in her condemnation, but neither was there any mercy. In her simple life she had kept unsophisticated the severe morality of a child, and it was this that judged him, that found him unpardonable and outlawed him" (p. 197). Later, after Hicks has left the *Aroostook*, Staniford reflects about Lydia that " 'Hicks being out of her world, her trust of everybody in it was perfect once more' " (p. 207). Lydia could only pity Hicks; but her compassion for him, the narrator observes, "was a religious duty." Staniford's generosity, on the other hand, "came easy to him." His temperamental generosity impels Staniford to save Hicks from the ocean the time Hicks fell overboard in the act of trying to strike Staniford. Lydia looks at Staniford's rescue as a case in which he merely did his duty: " 'when he struck at you so, you had to do everything.' " It is

Lydia's " 'Puritan conscience,' " Staniford reflects, " 'that takes the life out of us all.' "

In Venice, Lydia stays with her aunt, who advises her that there "a young girl mustn't go *any*where alone," not even to church. At first, Lydia does not understand. We would not expect her to in view of the innocence of her own view of herself in her situation aboard the *Aroostook*. But later, when her aunt asks Lydia to go with her to the Sunday night opera, Lydia is shocked. " 'Opera! Sunday night! Aunt Josephine, do you go to the theatre on Sabbath evening?' " We remember that Staniford, after hearing Lydia sing at Sunday morning service on the ship, thought of her as an "operatic novice." Once again, Howells, by cross-reference, complicates meaning in the novel by showing how attitudes and manners work to make the meaning of facts in experience. And at the center of the emerging complexity, "picturesquely," Howells says, is his American girl.

If Lydia had regarded her situation aboard the *Aroostook* as innocent in its nature, she soon learns that the wicked Old World takes quite another view of it.

> "Oh, I know what you mean, Aunt Josephine, but two days ago I couldn't have dreamed it! From the time the ship sailed till I reached this wicked place, there wasn't a word said nor a look looked to make me think I wasn't just as right and safe there as if I had been in my own room at home. They were never anything but kind and good to me. They never let me think that they could be my enemies, or that I must suspect them and be on the watch against them. They were Americans! I had to wait for one of your Europeans to teach me that. . . ." (p. 282)

In "passionate despair," says the narrator, Lydia continues:

"Oh, I see how my coming the way I have will seem
to all these people . . . I know how it will seem to that
married woman who lets a man be in love with her, and
that old woman who can't live with her husband because he's too good and kind, and that girl who swears
and doesn't know who her father is . . . and that
officer who thinks he has the right to insult women if he
finds them alone! I wonder the sea doesn't swallow up a
place where even Americans go to the theatre on the
Sabbath!" (pp. 282–83)

Lydia weeps now that Staniford may have only
been playing with her aboard the ship, only pretend-
ing to take an interest in her—" 'and he never meant
anything by anything.' " When Staniford does come
and confesses his love, Lydia hesitates. What did he
really think of her on the *Aroostook?* " 'I want to
know whether you were ever ashamed of me, or de-
spised me for it; whether you ever felt that because I
was helpless and friendless there, you had the right to
think less of me than if you had first met me here in
this house.' " This was, says the narrator, "a terrible
question, but it offered a loophole of escape, which
Staniford was swift to seize. Let those who will justify
the answer with which he smiled into her solemn
eyes: 'I will leave you to say' " (p. 314). It is all that
Lydia, triumphant in her innocence at the last, needs:
" 'Oh, I knew it, I knew it!' cried Lydia. And then, as
he caught her to him at last, 'Oh—oh—are you *sure* it's
right?' " Staniford answers that he does not doubt it.
"Nor," says the narrator, "had he any question of the
strategy through which he had triumphed in this cru-
cial test" (p. 315). It is a victory for both sides. Marry-
ing, Lydia and Staniford go to live in California!

The Lady of the Aroostook, says Olov W. Fryckstedt, "is a study in American innocence." [3] While it
is a study of American innocence, it is also a study of

its guilt. What Howells' novel shows is not the inherent superiority of America to a decadent Europe so much as a difference in perception of truth as it is formulated in the actualities of social conventions. Guilt comes in the self-righteousness which assumes that one's own view of things is the "real" one. In this sense the "vulgarity" which William Wasserstrom finds in Lydia [4] is not essentially different from that of others in the novel insofar as they take their own form of truth as absolute and exclusive. In Howells' satiric comedy virtue and vice, innocence and guilt are relative. The comprehensive point of view is pluralistic. Edwin Cady has rightly said that Howells uses "his perceptions of cultural and moral difference to give depth . . . to add dimension to the conventional-unconventional conflict. . . ." [5] Our customs and manners, Howells says, make up a large part of our identity —our recognition of who we are and what the world means. To recognize this identity is a step toward self-understanding, a step toward understanding our limitations. Perception of limitation makes possible the freedom for a broader perspective which recognizes the claims of worlds different from one's own. It is this union in difference that is symbolically hinted in the marriage of Lydia and Staniford.

IN HIS STUDY of Dr. Boynton, the spiritualist, in *The Undiscovered Country,* Howells once again reveals that human knowledge is limited and suggests that the morally humble life is the true one. Boynton, unsuccessful in his obsessive quest for knowledge about the spirit life and life after death, in the end asks forgiveness for his arrogance and finds peace in acceptance before his death. What he accepts is his dependance on others and his involvement with common life, recognizing that his own will and intentions are but a part of the life he shares with others. Without giving up his hope for some form of life after this one, he is yet able to accept that his power to know certain truth is limited by his human situation. Boynton, says Olov W. Fryckstedt, "becomes a symbol of man's eternally futile efforts to reach certainty about what happens to the human soul after death." [1] More immediately, however, what Howells shows is the uncertainty of knowledge about the world here and now; for it is this world that is the undiscovered country of his novel. As George N. Bennett notes, the marriage of Egeria—Boynton's daughter—and Ford, which closes the novel, is a "reduction of the problem of immortality to humanly possible terms." [2]

As the story opens Ford, a young man of scientific

and skeptical attitude, and his friend Phillips call upon Boynton in his Boston home to witness the latter's powers in spiritualism. Living with Boynton in a section of the city that is inhabited by fortune-tellers and charlatans is Egeria, her father's "medium." Boynton explains to Ford that he himself is seriously engaged in a quest for truth about the world of spirits. As for the charlatans, they represent, says Boynton, " 'an old tradition of supernaturalism,—a tradition as old as nature,' " and, he continues, " 'it seems to be a condition of our success that we shall not deny—I don't say that we shall believe—the fact of an occult power in some of them.' " [3] The problem the novel poses is that of the relationship between some kind of theoretical truth and reality and the truth in the facts of experience. Or, in other words, Howells, as a pragmatic realist, asks whether the facts point to some truth which transcends them. May actuality be explained by a transcendent "power"? If so, then the novel shows that that "power" is as various as its actual manifestations in the facts. Whatever knowledge Boynton seeks, he must find in the here and now.

As Boynton talks with Ford and Phillips, they are interrupted by a strange rapping in the woodwork of the walls and on a table top. Ford feigns indifference, but, suspecting quackery, keeps his eyes on Egeria. Boynton orders her to ask who is calling. She addresses the walls, asking whether it is "Giorgione?" An affirmative rapping comes from the woodwork. It is Giorgione, a Venetian painter of the Renaissance. Whether or not Giorgione is actually there in the woodwork, Egeria is "visibly" moved: "A thrill of strong excitement visibly passed over the girl. . . ." Just what it is that moves Egeria is not clear. At the end of the novel, for example, during the springtime, she enjoys a rebirth in health and spirit, as if she were somehow moved by the forces of nature. Also, she marries Ford, whose eyes are fixed on her here as the Renaissance spirit sounds from the walls. In bizarre humor, Howells' novel poses the riddle of meaning in facts.

An incident soon afterward deepens the mystery. Egeria, who dislikes spiritualism and her role as her father's medium, suddenly grows ill and excuses herself from a séance. Boynton goes out of the room with her. Ford then wryly remarks to his friend that Boynton will return presently " 'to say that our sphere—attitude, you call it; *his* quackery has a diffcrent nomenclature—has annulled his daughter's power over the spirits.' " Coming back, Boynton tells them they have just witnessed a mystery· " 'mystery, I call it, for I'm as much in the dark about it as yourselves. My daughter felt so deeply the dissenting, the perhaps incredulous, mood—sphere—of one of you that she quite succumbed to it' " (p. 15). Egeria will nonetheless take part in the séance, Boynton promises. He will "reinforce" her "powers" by his "mesmerism."

Boynton considers that the séance is a great success, even though Egeria, overcome, falls in a faint to the floor. Ford angrily threatens Boynton with exposure if the latter will not leave off his exhibitions. Indignant that his honesty should be questioned, Boynton proposes that a test séance be held in which he and Ford —as an opposing "sphere of influence"—may try who has the greater power over Egeria. Out of pity for Boynton, however, Ford declines. Soon afterward, Boynton and Egeria leave Boston for Maine, where conditions for studying the spirit world are more favorable. They mistake their train, though, and find themselves in Egerton. Here Boynton undergoes strange psychic disturbances and Egeria, caught in rain and snow, falls ill. They make their way to Vardley, Massachusetts, and the Shaker community there; and it is here that father and daughter eventually reconcile their differences and achieve a possible measure of happiness.

Before father and daughter recover their health—he in the spirit, she, in the body—both suffer a prolonged illness in the Shaker community. Among the Shakers, whose community was founded "to live the angelic life on earth," and whose ideals are celibacy and selflessness, Boynton at first believes he has found conditions that are perfect for him to carry on his investigations. He enthusiastically exclaims that the Shaker plan is the " 'only foundation on which a community can rest.' " Only gradually does Boynton become aware of the Shakers as embodying an influence adverse to his own purposes. For, caring only for the life of the spirit, Boynton scorns the Shakers' husbandry. Their notion that the angelic life of earth is proof of the spiritual world is repugnant to Boynton. The life of the spirit, he argues, is free of earth. Earth drags the spirit down. If they will but develop it, Boynton tells Elihu, a Shaker leader, the Shakers have in their government an ideal opportunity for a "perfect mediumship." Elihu replies: " 'You don't seem to realize that our very existence is a witness to the truth of an open relation between the spiritual and the material worlds. . . . We gave spiritualism to the world' " (p. 221). But Boynton argues that the Shakers have abused their gift by subordinating the life of the spirit to material interests. " 'I mean to make you think of your heavenly origin,' " he declares, " 'and realize how unworthy you have grown. You have subordinated your spiritualism to your Shakerism' " (p. 222). Elihu snorts that " 'Spiritualism was never anything but a means to Shakerism' "; and Boynton rejoins that he would " 'make it the end of Shaker-ism.' " The argument between Boynton and Elihu over Shakerism as "end" or "means" focuses on the central theme of the novel, the duality of man's na-ture in spirit and flesh as the chief problem of his existence. In effect, both Elihu and Boynton's atti-tudes oversimplify the metaphysical complexity of the human situation by their different and exclusive in-terpretations of it. The point the novel makes is that man lives in both worlds in his particularity and uni-versality and seeks continuously to reconcile fact and dream in his experience. At the end of the novel Boynton's peace consists in his acceptance of his hu-man situation, and that acceptance marks his healing in a ripeness that is complete, signified in his peaceful autumnal death.

Egeria's recovery among the Shakers is gradual and coincides with the coming of spring. "On the 20th of May . . . the consummate spring," Egeria leaves her bed and goes out of doors. With the season, she blos-soms into rich womanhood. She is aided in her recov-ery by the Shakers, who live close to the earth. They give her "herbs" and—ironically suggestive of fertility among the celibate Shakers—Sister Frances nurses Egeria with "maternal" tenderness. Egeria's strong at-traction to the Shaker life, in which she realizes her full womanhood, and Boynton's own defeat in the community which gave the world spiritualism, intensi-fies an ironic contrast of ideas that runs throughout the novel. With the coming of autumn, Egeria, no longer the pale and ethereal child of the beginning of the novel, stands before her father, her Northern fair-ness tinged with the South, "as the Young Ceres." Glancing at his daughter, Boynton, speaking out of his growing uneasiness among the Shakers, says: " 'I don't like my environment here . . . I am conscious of adverse influences.' " It is shortly after this comment that the quarrel between Boynton and Elihu occurs and precipitates a test séance in which Boynton boasts that he will prove his powers to the Shakers once and for all. Reluctantly, Egeria consents to act as her father's medium. The séance fails for Boynton. Egeria is no longer able to subject herself to his will, his "mesmeric force." A defeat for Boynton, the séance marks Egeria's delivery from his power.

Meanwhile, unknown to Boynton and Egeria, Ford and Phillips, making a kind of holiday tour in the country, have stopped at the Shaker community on the night of the test séance. Surprised when he later finds Ford there, Boynton, who has conceived Ford as an antagonistic influence, blames him for the failure of the séance and, enraged, seizes Ford as if to strangle him. At that moment, however, Boynton suffers a stroke from which he never recovers. The effects of this timely stroke have been well pointed out by Olov W. Fryckstedt: "But the stroke relieves Boynton from the terrible nervous tension under which he has labored. The sweet and kind sides of his nature gain the upper hand. He makes an effort to become reconciled to all the people he has hurt and treated unkindly." [4] Boynton's stroke, the means to his healing, must be included among the other forces and influences operating in the story; and, like them, must remain ambiguous in its final meaning. But whatever its ultimate meaning, the stroke effects Boynton's reconciliation with life and works for the good of all concerned. Giving up his obsession to know the absolute life of spirit, Boynton can accept life as a mixture of spirit and flesh, a metaphysical division in unity that is at once end and means in the fullness of existence.

Egeria's springtime rebirth and her father's repose in the autumn just prior to his death suggest the cyclical pattern of structure and theme in Howells' novel. Another implication is the notion of the complicity of all life. Ford, for instance, though not feeling himself directly responsible for Boynton's "misfortunes," yet feels that he is "somehow . . . entangled with him." Boynton himself says to Ford: " 'You have somehow been strangely involved in our destiny' " (p. 286). As a union of difference in complicity reconciliation is symbolically presented in the eventual marriage of Egeria and Ford. Egeria is at first troubled by their love, for she looks upon Ford as an antagonistic power and fears that he works some "spell" on her to bind her to him. On the contrary, Ford declares—he works no spell. He loves her, and he can take her love only with her free consent: " 'I loved you so that I couldn't have taken your love itself against your will! Ever since I first saw you, and all the time that I had lost you, my whole life was for you' " (p. 410). Oscar Firkins said that Ford's antagonistic influence turns out to be "not sorcery, but love." [5] Firkins is right; yet, love is one more instance of the essentially mysterious powers in the story; and if it is a reconciliation of opposing powers, then love is perhaps the greatest mystery of all. Life goes on, Howells says, in the union of Egeria and Ford; but their union, in its ultimate mystery, is the riddle of life's commonplace. The form of life and truth which Boynton sought denied the conditions of human existence which Egeria and Ford must live in. The last words are the narrator's:

> The grass has already grown long over Boynton's grave. They who keep his memory think compassionately of his illusions, if they were wholly illusions, but they shrink with one impulse from the dusky twilight through which he hoped to surprise immortality, and Ford feels it a sacred charge to keep Egeria's life in the full sunshine of our common day. If Boynton has found

the undiscovered country, he has sent no message back to them, and they do not question his silence. They wait, and we must all wait.

However it may be with Boynton, Egeria and Ford must live in the unknown world of the here and now. Living "in the full sunshine of our common day," they are one more instance of the realist's romance of real life.

EDWIN H. CADY has reported how William Dean Howells' search for a title for A *Modern Instance* ended
suddenly and happily with the novelist wiring his title
to Richard Watson Gilder, editor of *Century Magazine*, where Howells' novel first appeared in serial
form in 1882: "Then, at the last possible moment, the
phrase about the fat, pretentious justice of *As You
Like It*, 'full of wise saws and modern instances,'
drifted into Howells' mind, and he telegraphed his
title to Gilder." [1] The allusion in Howells' title to the
pretentious justice in Jacques' seven ages of man
speech, however, has a significance which has not yet
been recognized, for the title points to a central and
pervasive concern in Howells' novel. A *Modern Instance* is about the marriage and divorce of Marcia
Gaylord and Bartley Hubbard, but it has for a central
concern an inquiry into the nature of law and justice
in human experience. I do not mean law and justice
merely in a legal sense but in a moral sense as well. In
the last third of the novel, beginning with Chapter
XXVI, Ben Halleck and Eustace Atherton debate the
issue of whether experience ought to be evaluated on
the basis of a person's inner life or on the basis of his
actions. As it emerges in the novel, the issue comes
down to the question of whether motives or deeds

count more in judging experience. Halleck, who holds that motives count more, at one point speaks longingly to Atherton of " 'the relief, the rest, the complete exposure of Judgment Day.' " Atherton counters with the observation that " 'every day is Judgment Day.' " Impatient, Halleck replies: " 'Yes, I know your doctrine.' " [2] Atherton's doctrine is explicit later in the story in a speech to his wife as he moralizes about the broken marriage of Marcia and Bartley: " 'Oh, the meaning doesn't count! It's our deeds that judge us' " (p. 333). Howells' novel does not resolve the problem it raises. As William M. Gibson has observed, the novel's ending is "ironic, anticlimactic, and open" (p. xv). What the novel does conclude is that human pretentions to absolute law and justice, when not checked by an awareness of the limits of human knowledge, are unrealistic.

Although the motive-deed issue does not come into focus until late in the novel, it appears early and runs throughout. In Chapter VI, for example, Bartley Hubbard quarrels with Henry Bird and knocks him down, and Henry suffers a minor brain concussion when his head strikes the floor in his fall. To the doctor whom he summons, Bartley excuses himself on the grounds that he " 'never meant' " to strike Henry. " 'I didn't even intend to strike him when he hit me.' " However the doctor answers curtly that " 'intentions have very little to do with physical effects' " (p. 57). When Bartley afterwards explains to Mrs. Bird what happened, she cannot forgive him, and Bartley, unable to feel that he is guilty, complains to the doctor that Mrs. Bird is " 'very unjust' " (p. 59). Again, after Marcia has run away with Bartley and they are married and living in Boston, her father comes to visit her, and she begs him to "forgive" Bartley for the irresponsible way Bartley acted in the past. Squire Gaylord answers his daughter: " 'A man does this thing or that, and the consequence follows. I couldn't forgive Bartley so that he could escape any consequence of what he's done' " (p. 137). Of relevant interest is Howells' remark in a letter to T. W. Higginson that a point in A *Modern Instance* turns on the "irregularity" of Marcia's and Bartley's marriage (p. viii). Howells undoubtedly had in mind the quarrel between Marcia and Bartley in Chapter XXIX in which Bartley cruelly mocks Marcia's feeling that their marriage is "sacred."

> "Why—why—what do you mean, Bartley? We were married by a minister."
> "Well, yes, by what was left of one," said Bartley. "He couldn't seem to shake himself together sufficiently to ask for the proof that we had declared our intention to get married." (p. 256)

Though the minister was liable for his negligence to a sixty dollar fine, Bartley assures Marcia that they are, nonetheless, " 'married, right and tight enough,' " then concludes: " 'But I don't know that there's anything *sacred* about it.' " " 'No,' " cries Marcia, " 'it's tainted with fraud from the beginning' " (p. 257).

Finally, there are the incidents immediately leading up to the divorce trial and the climactic trial itself in an Indiana courtroom. The way in which notice of Bartley's suit for divorce reaches Marcia at Boston is a good example of Howells' extended use of the motive-deed issue. The newspaper carrying the required legal notice of Bartley's suit, after "a series of accidents and errors," its original address blurred beyond recognition, falls "by a final blunder" into the hands of Ben Halleck, who acting out of a sense of his duty, carries it to Marcia. Throughout the story Ben Halleck secretly loves Marcia, Atherton alone suspecting it. In-

terestingly, Halleck's secret love for Marcia, his argument with Atherton that Marcia after being abandoned by Bartley should divorce him (p. 317), and
Halleck's role in informing Marcia of Bartley's divorce
suit heighten the irony which grows with the development of Howells' story. In retrospect this irony is
seen to color the novel's meaning from its beginning.
Together, Marcia and her father, and Ben and his
sister Olive, leave by train for Indiana. En route Ben
confides to Olive that he is uneasy about Squire Gaylord's threats of "vengeance" against Bartley, and he
wonders whether Marcia has the same "motive."
Olive's reply is another variation and development of
the motive-deed issue which reaches to a consideration of divine motive at work in human events.
" 'We've got nothing to do with their motive, Ben.
We are to be her witnesses for justice against a wicked
wrong. I don't believe in special providences, of
course; but it does seem as if we had been called to
this work . . . that paper happening to come to you,
—doesn't it look like it?' " Halleck answers: " 'It
looks like it, yes' " (p. 337). Because their train is
delayed by an "accident," Marcia and the others arrive too late for the trial. The court, because it has
found Bartley's allegations true and because Marcia
has defaulted by failing to appear in time to defend
herself, has granted Bartley his divorce. However,
Squire Gaylord, who is a lawyer, asks and is granted
admission to the Indiana bar; and he requests that the
court set aside Marcia's default and grant her leave to
file a cross-petition for divorce. Addressing the court,
Squire Gaylord, whom Gibson aptly characterizes as
"a kind of Puritan atheist" (p. x), nonetheless, asserts
that he and his daughter are ready " 'to prove' " that
their right " 'is God's right, and the everlasting
truth' " (p. 353). Yet, when he goes on to declare that

he will seek the indictment of Bartley for perjury, Marcia cries out to her father to let Bartley go, and the Squire at that moment collapses from a stroke. Whatever the meaning of the stroke which fells Squire Gaylord, its effect on the old Puritan is clear: he is reduced to "the tremulous shadow of his former will" (p. 358). The novel's last picture of the Squire before his death, showing him sitting paralyzed in his Equity law office while his little granddaughter, Flavia, plays at his side, is moving in its ironic pathos: "He had become as a little child,—as the little child that played about him there in the still, warm summer days and built houses with his lawbooks on the floor" (p. 358).

The problem of the motive-deed issue is pointed in the novel's final scene. With Marcia divorced and widowed, Ben Halleck wonders whether he is not now free to ask her to marry him, and he writes to Atherton for advice. That Ben loved Marcia while she was Bartley's wife, however, seems " 'an indelible stain' " to Atherton, and he feels that for Ben to marry Marcia now could only " 'be loss,—deterioration,—lapse from the ideal' " (p. 362). Mrs. Atherton quickly points out to her husband, however, that he is judging Ben on his motive, and she reminds Atherton that he had " 'said the will didn't count.' " When she then asks him what he is going to do, Atherton, sighing, speaks the last words of the novel: " 'Ah, I don't know! I don't know'!" Because Ben Halleck represents for Atherton all that is good in civilized society, he sees a marriage between Ben and Marcia as striking at the roots of society's life. Forced to contemplate a marriage between Ben and Marcia, Atherton is unable to decide whether such an act should be viewed as legal, as moral, or as both. In brief, Atherton is forced to consider the problem of the meaning, that is, the motive of the act, and his dilemma makes clear an assumption implied throughout Howells' novel: the meaning of any act or physical event, of any fact, is not self-evident but depends, rathers on the point of view taken toward it. Howells, like his great contemporary realist, Henry James, was well aware of the importance of point of view in his fiction from the time of his earliest novels, and the careful attention both he and James gave to it marks their enlightened concern with the modern epistemological question of the real relationship between subject and object, mind and matter. Atherton's failure, finally, is one of perception. He does not see the limits of his knowledge; and for all his pretense to equity and justice, his doctrine is informed by his acute sense of his superiority as a member of good Boston society. Atherton after all must be set down as the justice in Howells' drama, and Atherton's portrait in the novel is one more Howellsian study of the New England Puritan in the nineteenth century.

That human knowledge about the real meaning of the forces operative in the visible world is limited, Howells' novel amply illustrates. The newspaper carrying the notice of Bartley's divorce suit which comes to Ben Halleck, the train "accident" which prevents Marcia from arriving at the trial in time to defend herself, the stroke which fells Squire Gaylord in the courtroom—these events belong, as much as Bartley Hubbard's striking of Henry Bird, among those physical effects in the novel which happen from no clear or certain motive. In *The Landlord at Lion's Head* (1897), Howells will again make use of the motive-deed issue, dramatizing it this time in the opposition between Jeff Durgin and Westover, who are variations of Bartley Hubbard and Atherton. When in one of their conversations Westover blames Jeff for being irresponsible in his conduct, Jeff replies that the trouble with Westover is that he assumes " 'that everything is done from a purpose, or that a thing is intended because it's done' "; but, Jeff concludes, " 'most things in this world are not thought about, and not intended. They happen, just as much as the other things that we call accidents.' " Jeff's observation that most things in life seem simply to "happen" could well be applied to A Modern Instance. Bartley's drifting into his engagement to Marcia; her sudden, runaway marriage to Bartley in which they failed to declare their intention of marriage to the minister; the irregularity of all their married life in its apparent irrationality of loving and quarrelling; Bartley's decision not to return to Marcia when he discovers that his money for a return ticket on the train has been stolen; the stunning and painful ironies of the climactic divorce trial: all these are instances in the novel of the way in which things seem simply to happen. Why they happen, what meaning ought to be ascribed to them remain mysterious. Although Howells does suggest that heredity, environment, training, and temperament share in the truth about the experience of his characters, he does not presume to interpret the significance of that experience or to judge his characters. The narrator's attitude toward the shooting of Bartley Hubbard is relevant. Bartley's death, the narrator observes, was a "penalty or consequence, as we choose to consider it, of all that had gone before" (p. 359).

The fatal shooting of Bartley Hubbard in Whited Sepulchre, Arizona by one of its "leading citizens"—Bartley "unfortunately chanced to comment upon the domestic relations" of that citizen—epitomizes in melodramatic violence the pretentious judgment of Bartley made throughout Howells' novel by the respectable people. Only Marcia, a tragic victim of the conflict between freedom and law, can speak out in the courtroom to let Bartley go. Society cannot let Bartley go, however, because his irresponsibility challenges the assumptions by which respectable society lives and tests their authenticity. Taking Bartley as the novel's symbol for the outlaw in life—his lawlessness is pointed by his failure to find his "basis" in law and by his increasing physical flabbiness—we see that the effect of his challenge to society is to reveal the falseness of its pretentions to righteousness and justice. The collapse of that facade is mirrored in Atherton's deflation at the last. The conclusion Howells' novel offers is that experience discloses no absolute law by which man may judge his experience. Consequently, he must judge it on the pragmatic basis of what seems best rather than on what he knows is best. What he believes is best he formulates into rules and laws. These are not final truths, however, but are provisional and are subject to change with man's changing life. In, thus, making the laws by which he orders his experience and gives it formal meaning, man invests his world with significant motive. Howells' implicit attitude toward law in his novel, interestingly, is similar to the one expressed by Justice Oliver Wendell Holmes in his *The Common Law*, a work published in 1881, just a year before Howells' novel appeared "The life of the law," Holmes wrotes, "has not been logic: it has been experience." [3] The awareness that man, in the face of his radically limited knowledge, must make his own meaning in life and that he is justified not by doing right but by his continuing effort to know what is right is the lesson of Howells' realistic modern instance.

BARTLEY HUBBARD'S INTERVIEW of Silas Lapham for
the *Events's* "Solid Men" series, which opens *The
Rise of Silas Lapham*, is a skillful compression of
thematic material and points toward its development
in the body of the novel. The opening scene, as
George Arms has observed, stands in pleasing symmetry with the closing one in which Sewell tests Lapham's sensibility.[1] Listening to Lapham tell his life to
Bartley, we become aware of a kind of conflict in
views between Lapham and Bartley out of which an
image of Lapham as a private person and public figure
emerges. George N. Bennett says that "the interview
is more than just a device of exposition by which
something of Lapham's past is revealed and certain
details of plot anticipated: it sets the steps for the
contrapuntal arrangement which will follow."[2] The
main business of the novel is in the harmonizing of
Lapham's private world with his public one, in affect-
ing a reconciliation between his intentions and his
actuality.

Bartley Hubbard conducts his interview of Lapham
in a manner that is in keeping with the advice given
him when he first went with the *Events*. At that time
Witherby had told Bartley that the interviews for the
"Solid Men" series were to be " 'guarded and inoffen-

sive as respects the sanctity of private life.' " [3] When in the course of the interview Lapham haltingly alludes to a partner he at one time had with him in his paint business, Bartley, forgetting for the moment his cynical manner, is alerted—he sniffs some hidden trouble. But Lapham does not go into the matter of the partnership. He "dropped the bold blue eyes with which he had been till now staring into Bartley's face, and the reporter knew that here was a place for asterisks in his interview, if interviews were faithful." Bartley understands "through the freemasonry of all who have sore places in their memories, that this was a point which he must not touch again."

Respecting what Witherby had called "the sanctity of the private life," Bartley sketches Lapham down as "a fine type of the successful American." But when Bartley at one point drops the remark that Lapham's life seems the "regulation thing," Lapham, from his personal view, is momentarily offended. He continues, however, proudly showing Bartley, says the narrator, a "standard" family photograph in which "decent, honest-looking, sensible people" had been arranged into "awkward and constrained attitudes." Bartley's news story on Lapham, we are told, "made a very picturesque thing" of the businessman's life. At the chapter's close its implications are summarized when Bartley refers to Lapham as that " 'old fool,' " and Bartley's wife, Marcia, exclaims: " 'Oh, what a good man!' "

Honest and decent people in constrained attitudes accurately suggests the comedy and pathos in the life of Lapham and his family. One thinks, for example, of the Laphams getting ready to attend the Corey dinner, of Silas' struggle to squeeze his huge hand into a white glove, and of the stylish house a Boston architect builds for Lapham. All these incidents function to point Lapham's grandiose and selfish intentions. The awkwardness in the Lapham family situation is further heightened by the triangular romance involving Irene and Penelope Lapham and Tom Corey.

Bartley Hubbard's mental substitution of asterisks for that part of Lapham's life which concerns a former business partner is a blot on Silas' record which Silas would overlook—if he could and if Mrs. Lapham would let him. Lapham had not wanted a partner with him in his paint business; and it was only after the war, when the day of "small" things in America seemed finished, that Lapham had given in to his wife and accepted Rogers and his money in partnership. Lapham, as he had told Bartley, had always felt that the paint which his father had found " 'was like my own blood,' " On Lapham's eventual deliverance from selfish pride depends his salvation. For it is Lapham's salvation that is at stake, and late in the novel Lapham's office clerk, Walker, and Lapham himself, employ a metaphor of shipwreck in regard to the foundering of Silas' prosperity. Walker says to Tom Corey about Rogers: " 'I guess that old partner of his has got pretty deep into his books. I guess he's over head and ears in 'em, and the old man's gone in after him, and he's got a drownin' man's grip round his neck.' " Silas attempts to cheer up his wife in their crisis, telling her: " 'A firm that I didn't think *could* weather it is still afloat, and so far forth as the danger goes of being dragged under with it, I'm all right' " (pp. 301–2). Silas has never wanted a partnership in his life's business, but one day, outside the new house he is building, Lapham and his wife meet Rogers. The chance encounter opens an old wound, and Lapham tries to explain once again to his wife that Rogers had had his choice of buying out or going out. Mrs. Lapham replies that it had been no choice at all: Silas knew that

Rogers could not have bought out at the time. When Lapham answers that, " 'It was a business chance,' " Mrs. Lapham answers: " 'No; you had better face the truth, Silas. It was no chance at all. You crowded him out. A man that had saved you!" ' (p. 48). At the end of the novel Rogers will provide the means by which Lapham discovers his involvement with others; thus, Rogers directly contributes to Lapham's ultimate moral salvation.

Lapham's ambitions have their effect on his family. Least susceptible by reason of her Puritanism—especially in the conscience she keeps as regards the Rogers business—is Mrs. Lapham; although, as George Arms points out, her husband's "social rise and the building of the house do not leave her stainless." It is in Lapham's daughters that their father's ambitions show themselves most markedly. Irene Lapham's belief that Tom Corey loves her rather than Penelope and the expectation of both the Lapham and Corey families that Tom will marry Irene suggest that both families are partly victimized by romantic conventions in which the socially inferior but beautiful girl marries the aristocratic young man. No one, however, is quite sure of Tom Corey's "intentions"; Tom isn't, himself. Lapham, though, says his wife, is determined that Irene and Tom will marry and " 'will move heaven and earth to bring it to pass.' " Bound by her sense of their past, however, Mrs. Lapham remains uneasy about her husband's intentions for himself and his family. She continues to fret about the old Rogers affair and, later in the novel, when that matter comes to a head, her rigidity will cause her to fail Silas when he needs her. Bound by the past and by a strict sense of duty, she will not be able to foresee the probable consequences of the course of action she would have Silas take in regard to Rogers and the Englishmen in their business deal.

If the romance between Irene and Tom seems forced, it is forced because the characters themselves behave in conventional ways which distort their actuality. Though Tom is never conscious of any clear intention toward Irene, she dreams of a love between them which, if realized, would fulfill romantic ideas of love. Irene is tainted by her father's ambitions, too. Even Penelope plays her part. Once it begins to appear that Tom loves Penelope rather than Irene, Penelope, in the manner of the sentimental heroine in *Tears, Idle Tears,* insists on sacrificing herself to the happiness of Tom and Irene—even though Tom does not love Irene. The situation is comic, but those involved suffer, and Silas and Mrs. Lapham are driven to seek help outside the family. They turn to Sewell, the minister. In a situation where none are to blame, he advises, it is better that one rather than three should suffer: " 'That's sense, and that's justice. It's the economy of pain which naturally suggests itself, and which would insist upon itself, if we were not all perverted by traditions which are the figment of the shallowest sentimentality' " (p. 257). Sewell's "economy of pain" formula, a justice tempered with mercy, appears in various guises throughout Howells' fiction.

Irene does not marry in the story, and her suffering over losing Tom leaves its mark on her; she toughens and loses "all her babyish dependence and pliability." Becoming more like her father, she reveals a "business-like quickness in comprehending" her father's affairs. Penelope and Tom, meanwhile, grow together in love and eventually are married—but their marriage comes only after Lapham himself begins to grow morally. Thus, the love between Penelope and Tom is a sign of the healing of the cancerous falseness which has infected the Lapham family. Howells prepares us for the union of Tom and Penelope by painting complementary traits in their characters. Tom, for instance, has not fitted into the pattern of his father's life. Bromfield Corey, Italianate aristocrat and dilettante artist, sees that Tom is more like Bromfield's dead father. For Tom has inherited his grandfather's Roman nose and the business energy of "the old India merchant, who had followed the trade from Salem to Boston when the larger city drew it away from the smaller." And Mrs. Lapham startles Mrs. Corey by telling her that in Mr. Lapham's opinion Tom is a " 'born' " businessman: " 'He says it's born in him to be a business man, and he can't help it' " (p. 179). Tom finds, too, that he is attracted to Penelope's fondness for books and to her quickness of wit. Complementary traits in Tom and Penelope facilitate their union, a symbolic joining of the lives of the Laphams and the Coreys, and hint at an organic continuity in experience in which all things work together. In this connection Edwin Cady has said:

> In planning *The Rise of Silas Lapham* in his notebook, Howells remembered an effective symbol from the frontier forest of his youth which he implied in the marriage of Tom and Penelope but did not see fit to quote in the final text of the book: "The young trees growing out of the fallen logs in the forest—the new life out of the old. Apply to Lapham's fall." [4]

The idea of life as an organic complicity is central in the novel. Lapham's own rise is a growth which joins him with the other life which surrounds him. At the last it is this interdependency of all existence which Lapham recognizes and is able to acknowledge. He sees then that all life is indeed a vast partnership business in which his own intentions make up a part. Silas, says Mrs. Lapham, never " 'meant wrong exactly' " in forcing Rogers out of the paint business; but Lapham did take advantage: " 'You had him where he couldn't help himself, and then you wouldn't show him any mercy,' " she tells him. Before Lapham achieves his true rise, he must see that, in the sum of the experience making up his life, he is not a "self-made" man. Others have shaped his life, as he has shaped their lives.

The turning point in Lapham's life comes in a business deal involving Rogers and some Englishmen. Now, Lapham is unable to act dishonestly in his own interest. The Englishmen, with Rogers as their agent, are willing to pay a good price for mill property held by Lapham. To sell would solve Lapham's present financial problems. Lapham has told the English representatives that the mill property in itself is of little value; it is dependent upon the railroad to get its produce to market, and the Great Lacustrine & Polar Railroad will be able to get the property for almost nothing. Knowing this, the Englishmen, who represent the interests of an "association of rich and charitable people," are, nonetheless, willing to buy the property as the site for an experiment in a new kind of community. The full implications of the situation have been pointed out by Donald Pizer:

> The crucial point is that the Englishmen are more than mere scoundrels and more than the agents for an "association of rich and charitable people"; they also represent society at large. This fact is somewhat obscured in the context of financial trickery involved in the sale, since the agents are willing to be cheated. But Howells indicated the social implications of the sale when he immediately compared it to the defrauding of municipal governments. In both instances wealth and anonymity encourage dishonesty, and in both instances dishonesty undermines that which is necessary for the maintenance of the common good—effective city governments on the one hand, fair play and honest deal-

ings in business affairs on the other. Lapham's refusal to sell therefore ultimately contributes to the wellbeing of society as a whole.[5]

In his struggle to decide what to do, Lapham gets little help from his wife. With the old business about Rogers still rankling in her conscience, she feels that Silas now has his chance to pay that debt in full by saving Rogers and his family in their time of need. " 'It does seem too hard,' " Mrs. Lapham says to her husband, " 'that you have to give up this chance when Providence had fairly raised it up for you.' " Lapham replies that he guesses " 'it wan't *Providence* raised it up.' " Lapham is unable to bring himself to sell the property; he sees that it would be dishonest to the interests represented by the Englishmen. Rogers pleads with Lapham to sell. " 'Can't you see,' " he says, " 'that you will not be responsible for what happens after you have sold?' " And Lapham answers that he " '*can't* see that.' " If in the past Lapham had acted selfishly in squeezing out Rogers, he is now unable to act either for his own or Rogers' interest because, as he sees it, the act would be dishonest. As Pizer points out, Lapham realizes that he cannot be dishonest with the men he expects to be honest with him. The suffering through financial loss which Lapham brings on himself and his family is not forced but is, rather, as Pizer has seen, a true economy of pain. The nature of the moral economy here, however, does not consist simply in the sacrifice of the good of the few to that of the many. For the loss of Lapham and his family is also their moral gain. Lapham's stand for honesty restores him to himself and to that larger humanity he shares with all other men. It is this, Sewell would say, that is "justice."

Lapham's ultimate rise, George Arms has said, comes "in the testing of his sensibility by Sewell. . . .

Now at last he refuses to indulge in overweening righteousness . . ." (p. xv). His ultimate rise is Lapham's
awareness of his interdependency with all life. Accord-
ingly, his view of his own importance is corrected by a
larger view of things and a sense of his own identity
within that complexity. At the last, Lapham humbly
accepts whatever responsibility may be his in the mysterious complicity that makes up existence.

In letting Lapham act as he must, Howells is true to
his conception of his character. Thus, method reveals
meaning in the novel as Lapham is tested by experience—all of this experience tells for meaning. Experience, as Howells sees it, is comprehensive and inclusive. " 'Nothing can be thrown quite away,' " as Sewell tells Lapham (p. 393). Organicism, continuity,
complicity—are principles of inclusion rather than exclusion.[6] What is included is one's idea of self in its
relation to other selves. These interact to make up a
plurality of worlds in which the individual and his
society share a common life. Howells' novel demon-
strates this organic inclusiveness not only in the relationship between Lapham and Rogers but in Lapham's broader development. Thus, theme is related to
structure in the organic totality of the novel. We have
already noted, for instance, the symmetry of the novel's structure in its opening and closing scenes where
Lapham's "solidity" is the subject. Details in both
episodes establish the organic concept of experience.
At the last, for example, Lapham tells Sewell that it
" 'seems sometimes as if it was a hole opened for me,
and I crept out of it.' " But it looks as if Lapham
always goes in at the same hole he comes out of. For
when Bartley had asked Lapham whether he had discovered the mineral paint on the farm himself, Lapham answered: " 'I didn't discover it. . . . My father
found it one day, in a hole made by a tree blowing

down. There it was, lying loose in the pit, and sticking to the roots that had pulled up a big cake of dirt with 'em. I don't know what give him the idea that there was money in it, but he did think so from the start' " (p. 5). And later, after Lapham has loaned Rogers money, and when he cannot meet business payments because others are not making their payments to him, Lapham tells his wife that it's going to be all right; then, he adds: " 'I ain't going to let the grass grow under my feet, though,—especially while Rogers digs the ground away from the roots' " (p. 279). Finally, there is the entry in Howells' notebook about the marriage between Penelope and Tom as representing new life growing out of the old.

Lapham's telling his wife that things are going to be all right hints lightly at a concept of fate that is variously expressed in the novel. On the other hand, fate is sometimes conceived as a form of Providence. We recall how Mrs. Lapham had thought that Providence had "raised up" a chance for her husband to rise morally by settling his old debt to Rogers. Then, there is the hereditary determinism of Lapham, his daughters, and of Tom and Bromfield Corey. Or there is the "chance" of the economic and social world. Or there is the chance world where "a hole made by a tree blowing down" turns up Lapham's fortune in life. Fate, Providence, heredity, character, chance—all are possible readings of the meaning of Lapham's experience. But to say that Providence *or* fate *or* character, and so on, satisfactorily explains Lapham's story is to reduce the complex reality of Lapham's world. At the last, Lapham does not presume to judge his guilt or innocence. He accepts the limitations of his knowledge and of his own importance. Insofar as he had lived for himself and his own purposes exclusively, he falsified his situation. Mrs. Lapham, too, was bound too fast by her Puritanism and the past, while her husband tried to ignore his past by living for the future. Both Lapham and his wife, in their mutual crisis, learn that there is more to life and to their own lives than they had allowed. In the Rogers affair Mrs. Lapham sees "that she had kept her mind so long upon that old wrong which she believed her husband had done this man that she could not detach it, but clung to the thought of reparation for it when she ought to have seen that he was proposing a piece of roguery as the means" (pp. 359–60). And Lapham, in that healing which is his growth of self and which is brought about by his acceptance of the larger implications of his experience, lives in the end on the Vermont farm where he had his beginning.

Howells' moral vision in *The Rise of Silas Lapham* is one in which all men share responsibility together in their complicity. Lapham's achievement of honesty is in his acceptance of all sides of his experience—inward and outward, private and public. Nothing is quite lost nor can it be thrown away. Morality is emergent in this process and is not a fixed code or convention to be followed without regard to the felt necessities of particular situations. The moral view, in brief, is pragmatic. In his introduction to the novel, Everett Carter writes:

> Howells tried to show in his fiction the operation of a moral system, flexible and changing to meet changed conditions and involved with people organized into functioning societies; he demonstrated that to keep to oneself is spiritually to die, to give oneself to others is spiritually to live; he used fiction to show the operation of 'a force, not ourselves, that works for righteousness.' In brief, this was Emerson's vision fused with the hardheadedness of the empirical tradition from Locke to Comte, and, as it evolved in the American nineteenth

century, given the name of 'pragmatism.' What works is right; not what works in the short arid stretch of personal gain, but what works for people organized into societies.[7]

And Donald Pizer has said "that the ethical core of the novel can be described as utilitarianism (as interpreted by John Stuart Mill). . . ." [8]

True ideas, said William James, are made in experience. Ideas "become true just in so far as they help us to get into satisfactory relations with other parts of our experience. . . ." [9] In *The Rise of Silas Lapham* it is Lapham's getting into satisfactory relations with other parts of his experience that constitutes his growth. At the novel's close his acceptance of his experience in a spirit of humility marks his true stature. He says: " '. . . if I done it, and the thing was to do over again, right in the same way, I guess I should have to do it.' "

WHILE CRITICAL COMMENT about *Annie Kilburn* has dealt for the most part with the novel's social and economic problems, a wider view of the novel is helpful in understanding its larger concerns. These are brought out in the education of Annie Kilburn, an idealistic but self-centered young lady who has an obsession to do good for others. It is not poverty nor social and economic injustice that is the theme of *Annie Kilburn*. "The follies of the charitable," rather, as Oscar Firkins has noted, is the theme.[1] Howells' comedy of a young New England lady who wants to do good reveals that the impulse to be charitable to others while denying the claims of one's self can be a subtle form of selfishness. Annie Kilburn learns something like a natural economy of charity when she discovers that to do good truly is to do it for one's self as well as for others. The two are closely related, and it is within this framework she finds that a genuine basis for social union exists.

Annie's journey from Rome to Hatboro, Massachusetts, is one that leads her from the emptiness of romantic dreaming to fulfillment in reality. Some such development is indicated by the narrator early in the novel.

She had felt, as every American of conscience feels abroad, the drawings of a duty, obscure and indefinable, toward her country, the duty to come home and do something for it, be something in it. This is the impulse of no common patriotism; it is perhaps a sense of the opportunity which America supremely affords for the race to help itself, and for each member of it to help all the rest.[2]

Annie comes home, says Edwin Cady, "to fulfill the American Dream—our democracy is the last, best hope of earth. . . ."[3] But, as Cady also observes: "At home in Hatboro, Massachusetts, Annie finds it immensely more difficult to do good than she had supposed."[4] Annie's intentions are admirable. The novel shows, though, that intentions must deal with complex actualities in the conflicts of experience. The idea of "good" in the story is differently conceived by different persons. Conflicts over what is good, act to separate individuals, for example, the situation between the practical Mr. Gerrish and the impractical Reverend Mr. Peck. Democracy in *Annie Kilburn* is complexly inclusive and embraces the differing points of view of persons like Gerrish and Mr. Peck without absolutely accepting either one. Annie's education prepares her to perceive life's complicity. Returning to Hatboro, Annie at first is able to see only the differences among persons in what Cady calls "sadly complex and warring Hatboro." The forms of selfishness, it appears, are radical as the differences between men and women. But just as the sexes go together in the economy of nature, so in Hatboro forms of unity seek expression in the midst of alienations and differences. That selfishness exaggerates differences among men at the expense of their common life is a theme throughout Howells' fiction. For Howells, self-pride often expressed itself in manners. He puts it succinctly in *The*

Rise of Silas Lapham: ". . . it is certain that our manners and customs go for more in life than our qualities. The price we pay for civilization is the fine, yet, impassable differentiation of these. Perhaps we pay too much; but it will not be possible to persuade those who have the difference in their favor that this is so." [5]

Among those in Hatboro who have the difference in their favor is Annie. As one of the old Hatboro Kilburns, she enjoys the superiority of an aristocratic family tradition. It is not quite accurate to say that Annie enjoys her superiority, though; for it is just that superiority which she feels as part of her problem. Only when she understands that superiority as something different from what she had imagined will she be able to rest in it. As for superiority, everyone in Hatboro shows some form of it. Notable among the varieties for its quality of toughness is that of Mrs. Munger. Dressed in clothes that are rigged with "leather," Mrs. Munger, who "might be said to be in harness," rides through Hatboro spreading the word about her proposed plan for a Social Union on behalf of the town's poor working classes. Annie, though somewhat uneasily, rides with her. It is not quite what Annie had expected, but it will do until something more really ideal presents itself.

Something more really ideal presents itself in the person of the Reverend Mr. Peck, and, though differently, in his little girl, Idella. Peck's is a somewhat chilling superiority on those austere heights from which he looks pityingly down on the selfishness which divides a competitive Hatboro. His sympathies are for the poor; his severities are for the well intentioned but superfluous charities of the offensive rich. Not charity but justice is what the world needs, he preaches. Where justice prevails, the evil of social and

economic differences among men will vanish because
selfishness will have been replaced by a triumphant
equality. He says in a sermon:

> Charity is the holiest of the agencies which have
> hitherto wrought to redeem the race from savagery and
> despair; but there is something holier yet than charity,
> something higher, something purer and further from
> selfishness, something into which charity shall willingly
> grow and cease, and that is *justice*. Not the justice of
> our Christless codes, with their penalties, but the in-
> stinct of righteous shame which, however dumbly, how-
> ever obscurely, stirs in every honest man's heart when
> his superfluity is confronted with another's destitution,
> and which is destined to increase in power till it be-
> comes the social as well as the individual conscience.
> Then, in the truly Christian state, there shall be no
> more asking and no more giving, no more gratitude and
> no more merit, no more charity, but only and evermore
> justice; all shall share alike, and want and luxury and
> killing toil and heartless indolence shall cease together.
> (p. 240)

It is during this sermon that Hatboro's leading merchant, William Gerrish, rises from his pew and, his
family trailing after him, marches indignantly from
the church. Standing for a rugged individualism, as he
believes, Gerrish has no patience with Peck's idea of
the Christian state in its communal selflessness and
absolute equality. The opposing extremes of the two
positions suggest something of the moral situation
which Annie learns to deal with in the novel. In the
end, though she still is attracted to Peck's ideal, Annie
loves Dr. James Morrell, whose practical experience as
a physician has made him the kind of man to serve as
a balance for Annie's own impracticality. Annie and
Morrell, recalling Peck after his death, talk of Annie's
relationship to Peck. She says to Morrell: " 'I could

have worshipped him, but I couldn't have loved him — any more,' she added, with an implication that entirely satisfied him, 'than I could have worshipped *you.*' "

Within the total context of the novel's view of life, Peck's doctrine of selfless equality and the raw individualism of Gerrish are narrow in their righteousness. Both views have to be taken into account in making up the sum of experience. Early in the novel Mrs. Bolton tells Annie that if Peck kept more of his money for himself instead of giving it to others, he could dress Idella better. " 'Oh, that's the way with these philanthropists,' said Annie thinking of Hollingsworth, in *The Blithedale Romance*, the only philanthropist whom she had really ever known. 'They are always ready to sacrifice the happiness and comfort of any one to the general good' " (pp. 67–68). Following Peck's death—he is struck down and killed by a train on the tracks dividing Hatboro—the feeling of the townspeople toward Peck is expressed by the narrator: "They revered his goodness and his wisdom, but they regarded his conduct of life as unpractical. They said there never was a more inspired teacher, but it was impossible to follow him" (p. 317). It is worth noting that Peck's wife died insane; and, we learn, he had left his parish in Maine largely because he had made life unbearable for the average parishioner.

Howells' satire reduces Gerrish's viciousness so that it seems harmless enough. His is a travesty of individualism as he lays down his rules for the business of life to Mrs. Munger in her leathery resistance. Perched on a stool in his office, gesturing with a ruler in hand, Gerrish preaches his sermon. People, he exclaims, have got to learn their place: " 'You've got to put your foot down, as Mr. Lincoln said; and as *I* say, you've got to *keep* it down' " (p. 83). Gerrish will have no part of Peck's doctrine of equality. Christ did not mean that men should actually be equal. What counts, Gerrish declares, is the intention to be Christ-like insofar as " 'circumstances will permit.' " Gerrish is right, but he is wrong, too. Intentions are to be counted; but the problem which Gerrish skirts, is in the reconciliation of intentions with "circumstances."

In Hatboro, Annie is struck by her observation that all her good intentions to help others are frustrated by a people who seem "terribly self-sufficing." Late in the novel she reflects that "of her high intentions, nothing had resulted." An inexorable centrifugality Annie learns to face in the people of Hatboro—as well as in herself. Annie's particular kind of selfishness is her obsession to do good and her Puritan presumption which instructs her that evil but not good comes from her own impulses and wishes. Any good in her can only be from God. The ironic implications of her attitude are pointed in the narrative.

> She had always regarded her soul as the battlefield of two opposite principles, the good and the bad, the high and the low. God made her, she thought, and He alone; He made everything that she was; but she would not have said that He made the evil in her. Yet her belief did not admit the existence of Creative Evil; and so she said to herself that she herself was that evil, and she must struggle against herself; she must question whatever she strongly wished because she strongly wished it. It was not logical; she did not push her postulates to their obvious conclusions; and there was apt to be the same kind of break between her conclusions and her actions as between her reasons and conclusions. She acted impulsively, and from a force which she could not analyse. She indulged reveries so vivid that they seemed to weaken and exhaust her for the grapple with realities; the recollection of them abashed her in the presence of the facts. (pp. 8–9)

If Howells' novel is concerned about the differences among men which divide them socially, notice is given here that there are divisions within individuals themselves. Annie's conflict between her intentions to do good and her desire to please herself is focused in her conduct toward Peck's little girl, Idella. Idella serves as a reminder that the ideal level of existence aspired to by her father lacks a common sense essential to man's more mundane life. Clothed almost in rags, Idella suffers the effects of her father's impractical altruism. Annie, showing an instinctive maternal compassion for Idella, buys her a new dress and hat. Toward these wordly things Idella, raised by her father to live a life of self-denial, shows a "primitive" and "greedy transport." If Idella is to live, Howells seems to say, she must at least have the things of this world. Annie's growth in love for Idella is a part of Annie's education; it balances her abstract idealism and fills it out in the concrete instance. At the same time it helps prepare the way for her union with Dr. Morrell.

The novel's most forceful illustration of man's conflict with himself is seen in Ralph Putney, a lawyer whose law suffers from his alcoholism. Coming from a fine Hatboro family, equipped with a keen mind, and having had an excellent education, Putney might have gone on to a brilliantly successful career if it were not for his periodic drinking. Putney's "infirmity" is his division against himself in his continuing struggle to live a balanced life. His conflict and struggle make Putney seem intensely real along side of other one-dimensional characters like Gerrish, Mrs. Munger, and perhaps even Peck and Annie herself. Putney's infirmity causes him to swing from one extreme in himself to another as he struggles to be a whole man. Mrs. Putney says of him that he only keeps " 'within bounds at all . . . by letting himself perfectly loose.' " Containing within his own experience conservatism and liberalism, wealth and poverty, selfishness and selflessness, Putney is a microcosm of Hatboro. That Howells meant Putney to reflect the community's own conflict is explicit. We learn from Dr. Morrell, for example, that Putney has a chance of winning his fight with himself, and near the close of the novel the narrator links Putney's fate with that of Hatboro's Social Union. "Putney studies its existence in the light of his own infirmity, to which he still yields from time to time, as he has always done. He professes to find there a law which would account for a great many facts of human experience otherwise inexplicable. He does not attempt to define this occult preservative principle, but he offers himself and the Social Union as proofs of its existence; and he argues that if they can only last long enough they will finally be established in a virtue and prosperity as great as those of Mr. Gerrish and his store" (p. 327).

The founding of the Peck Social Union is indirectly owing to Dr. Morrell. It is he who urges Annie to go on with the idea for a Social Union after everyone else has given it up. Morrell suggests to Annie that, after all, it could perhaps do some good. If the Peck Social Union is not all Annie intended—"its working is by no means ideal"—she, nonetheless, finds that she is able to be of real use. It is a limited use, though, and reminds Annie of her own limitations.

> She has kept a conscience against subsidising the Union from her own means; and she even accepts for her services a small salary, which its members think they ought to pay her. She owns this ridiculous, like all the make-believe work of rich people; a travesty which has no reality except the little sum it added to the greater sum of her superabundance. She is aware that she is a pensioner upon the real members of the Social

Union for a chance to be useful, and that the work they
let her do is the right of some one who needs it. She has
thought of doing the work and giving the pay to another; but she sees that this would be pauperising and
degrading another. So she dwells in a vioious circle, and
waits, and mostly forgets, and is mostly happy. (pp.
326–27)

Howells' novel offers no easy solutions to the problems of a complexly divided Hatboro. In the town's
production of *Romeo and Juliet*, their version of it
reduced to a banality in which there could be "no
possible offense," Howells hints that oversimplifica-
tion of the novel's problems is a matter of amateur
theatricals. Annie Kilburn came home to Hatboro
with high intentions of doing good only to learn how
difficult it is to do good at all. Wherever she would
take hold, she found herself repelled by the "inexorable centrifugality" of a terrible self-sufficiency, not
the least of which was her own. Good intentions,
Annie discovers, are not enough; one has to deal with
actualities as they assert themselves in others and in
oneself. The problem is to understand with any certainty, however, just what the actualities mean.
Annie, we recall, had thought that the good in her was
from God, and the evil, from herself; but she has been
able to do little good in Hatboro, and surely her desire
to care for Idella could not be evil? The townspeople
are inclined to think that Peck had been thwarted by
death in his intentions for Idella. They see his death
as a "sign" that he had been wrong, and conclude that
Idella has been given to Annie "for some purpose
which she must not attempt to cross" (p. 318). Later,
when Annie is about to give up the whole idea of a
Social Union and complains to Morrell that the business has been left in her unwilling hands, he suggests
that perhaps " 'it's a sign you're not intended to get

rid of it' " (p. 323). Peck's death, remarks the narrator, "was in no wise exegetic." His death "said no more to his people than it had said to Annie; it was a mere casualty; and his past life, broken and unfulfilled, with only its intimations and intentions of performance, alone remained" (p. 317).

In the pluralistic experience of the realist's world, absolute certainty about the meaning of facts is not possible. Where certainties are elusive, a one-sided view of the meaning of experience is necessarily only partial in truth. Life means different things to different people. A humorous illustration of the idea comes in an incident in Annie's tour of the Wilmington factory. Lyra Wilmington shows Annie the rooms where stockings are stamped with different numbers, indicating size. Lyra says to Annie: " 'The stockings are all one *size*, Annie; but people like to wear different numbers, and so we try to gratify them' " (p. 150). Late in the novel, narrative, comment about a too rigid point of view is explicit. "One of the dangers of having a very definite point of view is the temptation of abusing it to read the whole riddle of the painful earth" (p. 328). Mrs. Munger, Mr. Gerrish, Reverend Mr. Peck, "near-sighted" Annie: all have more or less fixed points of view. Among the characters, Dr. Morrell is least insistent about his own view. Near the end of the novel, for instance, when Annie feels that she holds an "unswerving allegiance" to Peck's philosophy, she is troubled by Dr. Morrell's attitude. She is puzzled that Morrell, while admitting the force of her reasoning about Peck and his ideas, "should be content to rest in a comfortable inconclusion as to his [own] conduct." One day it suddenly dawns on Annie, however, "that this was what she was herself doing, and that she differed from him only in the openness with which she proclaimed her opinions" (p. 329).

The correction of Annie's nearsightedness in the novel is gradual. There is one moment, however, when she has a flash of perception that permits us to think her education has not been in vain. The moment comes near the novel's end, just after Morrell has told Annie that Idella is through the crisis of a lung-fever and is going to be well again.

She [Annie] remained at her door looking up at the summer blue sky that held a few soft white clouds, such as might have overhung the same place at the same hour thousands of years before, and such as would lazily drift over it in a thousand years to come. The morning had an immeasurable vastness, through which crows flying across the pasture above the house sent their voices on the spacious stillness. A perception of the unity of all things under the sun flashed and faded upon her, as such glimpses do. Of her high intentions, nothing had resulted. An inexorable centrifugality had thrown her off at every point where she tried to cling. Nothing of what was established and regulated had desired her intervention; a few accidents and irregularities had alone accepted it. But she now felt that nothing withal had been lost; a magnitude, a serenity, a tolerance intimated itself in the universal frame of things, where her failure, her recreancy, her folly, seemed for the moment to come into true perspective, and to show venial and unimportant, to be limited to itself, and to be even good in its effect of humbling her to patience with all imperfection and short-coming, even her own. She was aware of the cessation of a struggle that has never since renewed itself with the old intensity; her wishes, her propensities, ceased in that degree to represent evil in conflict with the portion of good in her; they seemed so mixed and interwoven with the good that they could no longer be antagonised; for the moment they seemed in their way even wiser and better, and ever after to be the nature out of which good as well as evil might come. (pp. 319–20)

Annie's vision of life's vast interdependency, its unity in multiple difference, is a version of Howells' complicity. Within this large perspective that flashes and fades, Annie achieves a finer and truer understanding of herself. She sees now that her intentions, noble as they may have been, made but a thread in life's vast tapestry of experience where all things are interwoven. Within the complexities of this pattern, no single-mindedness of view can hope to trace an ultimate design as the meaning of the whole. What is possible, however, is an intelligent effort to broaden one's view to include as much within it as one can. Only continued effort to achieve more generous perspectives can furnish a better charity and justice in human conduct than those partially urged as the whole truth in *Annie Kilburn*.

A HAZARD OF NEW FORTUNES (1890), called by Howells the "largest canvas" he had yet allowed himself,[1] explores the American social and economic scene as it appeared in the New York of the later nineteenth century. Yet, the novel is not mere fictionalized sociology, as recent commentators have made clear. George Arms, for example, emphasizes that the novel is in the tradition of the comedy of manners as exemplified by Jane Austen, and that it achieves its end "through comic insight and without dogmatic persuasion." Everett Carter acclaims the novel's "autobiographic mode" in which, by "selection and arrangement" of material, Howells transformed his own experience into the "reality" of fiction; and Carter finds in the "deeper meaning" of the story a strong hint of the Christian "myth" of man's fall and his hoped-for redemption. George N. Bennett, while objecting to what he feels is a lack of organic unity in the novel, nonetheless, finds it a provocative study of the relation between character and circumstance. And Edwin H. Cady, in the "fall of Jacob Dryfoos," sees Howells as writing a moving "realistic tragedy" in which tragic events are "embedded in relatively nontragic events."[2] Howells' novel, then, goes beyond social and economic concerns while including them at the same time; and, if the novel's title points to the overt theme of the story, it points also to the larger theme of the risk of living in a world where fortune is always uncertain in the complicity of experience.

The novel is divided into five parts. In the first three we meet the characters, have views of New York, and watch the interweaving of the lives of the characters whose fortunes are involved with the launching of the new magazine *Every Other Week*. The people associated with the magazine form a microcosm of the greater world. Basil March, the magazine's literary editor and the novel's central character, is a Westerner, as are Fulkerson, the magazine's genial director, and Jacob Dryfoos, a "natural-gas" millionaire who is the magazine's "Angel." Its art editor, Angus Beaton, the son of a tombstone cutter and "Scotch Seceder," is from Syracuse, New York. Colonel Woodburn, a contributor, is from Charlottesburg, Virginia. In Berthold Lindau, the old German socialist who translates European literature for the magazine, *Every Other Week* takes on an international flavor. Other characters whose fortunes are involved with those of the magazine include Mrs. March, a Bostonian; Mrs. Leighton and her artist daughter, Alma, from St. Barnaby, New Hampshire; Margaret Vance, an altruistic young lady of New York society; Miss Woodburn, the Colonel's daughter and eventual wife of Fulkerson; and, finally, Conrad Dryfoos, old Dryfoos' son and the magazine's publisher.

The conflict of the novel, as George Arms has observed, appears in part three when March, anticipating his first meeting with Dryfoos, experiences a "disagreeable feeling of being owned and of being about to be inspected by his proprietor" (p. 234). This incipient conflict erupts in part four when March refuses to submit to Dryfoos' dictatorial command that Lindau be fired from *Every Other Week*. In part five of the novel the conflict expands outward to society in the New York street car strike, and it reaches its climax in the riot in which Conrad Dryfoos is shot and killed.

To comprehend the scope and nature of the conflict in Howells' novel, however, it must be viewed in contexts other than the economic one, and to do this task we need to look at the history of some of the characters. Howells' story suggests, for example, that perhaps there is some kind of necessity or determinism which runs through things. At the beginning of the novel, when he is urging March to come on to New York as literary editor of *Every Other Week*, Fulkerson reminds March that he has never liked the insurance business—" 'it's killing you. You ain't an insurance man by nature. You're a natural-born literary man, and you've been going against the grain. Now, I offer you a chance to go *with* the grain' " (p. 3). The implication is that March, somehow, is meant to be a literary man, and March himself tells us that he had "early literary ambitions" (p. 15). Conrad Dryfoos had wanted to be a minister, but his inclination all along had been thwarted by his father, who was determined to make a business man of him. Yet, after Conrad's death, Dryfoos talks to Angus Beaton.

> "My son, he wanted to be a preacher, and I did stop *him*—or I thought I did. But I reckon he was a preacher, all the same, every minute of his life. As you say, it ain't any use to try to stop a thing like that. I reckon if a child has got any particular bent, it was given to it; and it's goin' against the grain, it's goin' against the law, to try to bend it some other way." (514)

The key words here are, of course, "bent," "grain," and "law." The implication is again the same: that perhaps some necessity or determinism runs through things. What the character of this determinism is, Howells' novel does not finally say. Perhaps it is a naturalistic determinism, as "bent" and "grain" suggest. Or, as Dryfoos, speaking out of some residue of an earlier Calvinism, suggests, perhaps the determinism is a divine predestination. Through March and Conrad, Howells lets us see that one's vocation, one's calling, may not be viewed merely in terms of social or economic circumstance, though that circumstance, too, can not be ignored.

However, it may also be that chance operates in things. Returning again to the beginning of the novel, we hear March tell Fulkerson that " 'it was more an accident than anything else that I got into the insurance business' " (p. 4). When, in chapter two, March sounds his wife about Fulkerson's "scheme" for the new magazine, she asks her husband: " 'But what have you got to do with it?' " March's reply not only suggests the operation of chance in things, it includes the idea of a possible inevitability in his fortune.

> "It seems that Fulkerson has had his eye on me ever since we met that night on the Quebec boat. I opened up pretty freely to him, as you do to a man you never expect to see again, and when I found he was in that newspaper syndicate business I told him about my early literary ambitions" (pp. 14–15).

Moreover, it turns out, according to Fulkerson, that the idea for the magazine came originally from March himself when the two men met, apparently by chance, years ago. Anticipating March's moral stand against the capitalist Dryfoos later in the story, we do well to take note here of the kind of magazine March envisioned to Fulkerson at their first meeting. March says to his wife:

"When he told me about his supplying literature to newspapers for simultaneous publication, he says I asked: 'Why not apply the principle of co-operation to a magazine, and run it in the interest of the contributors?'" (p. 15)

Thus, March's antipathy for Dryfoos before meeting him has roots in March's past. Determinism and chance seem to have cooperated in the making of March's fortune, as they seem to have in the making of the fortune of *Every Other Week*. Just prior to the appearance of the first number of the magazine, March reflects about recent events.

It seemed to him that there were no crazy fortuities that had not tended to its existence, and as time went on, and the day drew near for the issue of the first number, the sense of this intensified till the whole lost at moments the quality of a waking fact, and came to be rather a fantastic fiction of sleep.

Yet the heterogeneous forces did co-operate to a reality which March could not deny, at least in their presence, and the first number was representative of all their nebulous intentions in a tangible form. (p. 211)

When, from the vantage point of the end of Howells' novel, we look back to the beginning and hear March tell his wife—Fulkerson "'says he owes it all to me; that I invented the idea—the germ—the microbe'" (p. 15), the rich irony of the novel's complicity strikes us forcefully.

In addition to a possible determinism and chance as operative in things, there is also individual volition. Our sense of Jacob Dryfoos in the novel is of a man of strong will. He would rule, both in his private and public affairs, with a sure hand. One of Howells' favorite images for the man of will is that of the horse driver (cf. Silas Lapham), and it appears at least three times in the novel in connection with Dryfoos. March applies it to Dryfoos just after his meeting with him: "'the man that holds the purse holds the reins'" (p. 244); Dryfoos uses it to his wife about himself: "'Mr. Fulkerson can bear a little watching now. He's been travelling pretty free, and he's got the notion he's driving, maybe'" (p. 254); and Fulkerson, flattering Colonel Woodburn to get him to go to Dryfoos to act as mediator in the trouble between Dryfoos and March, says to the Colonel: "'you're the man on horseback to him; and he'd be more apt to do what you say than if anybody else said it'" (p. 413). Angus Beaton, who furnishes Fulkerson with the idea and the image, perceives that Dryfoos' attraction to the Virginia Colonel is the latter's advocacy of a system of "'patriarchal slavery'" (p. 407). Jacob Dryfoos' role as the man of will and as the patriarch has rich implication in the novel. Early in it, for example, Fulkerson, telling March how Dryfoos left his Indiana farm and got into the natural-gas business, half jokingly remarks that Mrs. Dryfoos backed her husband all the way. "'She thought whatever he said and did was just as right as if it had been thundered down from Sinai'" (p. 91). But our sense of Jacob Dryfoos as a man of righteous will comes most forcefully from his lording it over his obedient and gentle son; and when, in the climactic scene between the two, Jacob strikes his son, wounding him "in his temple" with Christine Dryfoos' intaglio ring, and Conrad, in "grieving wonder," exclaims, "'Father!'" the implications of significance are fertile indeed. As Everett Carter has suggested, the episode carries with it strong overtones of the Biblical Hebraic and Christian myths.[3]

Believing his cause justified by the pile of money he amasses, Dryfoos preaches his gospel of self-sufficiency to Conrad: "'You know . . . what work and saving and steady habits and sense will bring a man to'" (p.

238). This, too, in spite of his occassional feeling that his fortune works against him. At one point he tells his wife:

> "I don't say we're any better off, for the money. I've got more of it now than I ever had; and there's no end to the luck; it pours in. But I feel like I was tied hand and foot. I don't know which way to move; I don't know what's best to do about anything. The money don't seem to buy anything but more and more care and trouble. We got a big house that we ain't at home in . . . Our children don't mind us . . . But it had to be. I couldn't help but sell the farm, and we can't go back to it, for it ain't there." (pp. 254–55)

Nonetheless, Dryfoos' false sense of his righteousness is what moves him, and in the final scene between him and his son, it is his righteousness which lashes out when Conrad says to his father of the streetcar strikers: " 'I believe they have a righteous cause' " (p. 465). His son's death is a crushing blow to Dryfoos, and it breaks his fierce pride and his will. Our last view of him as he prepares to embark for Europe with his family is of a man "wearied and bewildered" by what he has come to. Before Dryfoos leaves New York, he sells *Every Other Week*, "the thing," he calls it, after the manner of Fulkerson—sells "the thing" to Fulkerson and March, and March is thrilled by the "wonderful good-fortune as seemed about falling to him" (p. 535). At the last, then, March does have his magazine, the magazine which, we recall, was his idea in the first place. In another way, too, Howells at the last humorously points the organic symmetry of his story in which diverse fortunes yet are one. Married now to Miss Woodburn, Fulkerson goes with her "down the St. Lawrence to Quebec over the line of travel that the Marches had taken on their wedding journey. He had the pleasure of going from Montreal to Quebec on the same boat on which he first met March" (p. 550).

Free will, chance, necessity: all seem at work in what the novel shows as the complicity of experience. Experience itself is neutral, however, and it takes on significant form only as the characters themselves give it form out of their needs, their beliefs, and their acts. Angus Beaton in the novel, by turns a painter, a writer, a sculptor; a man who in doing whatever he likes finally does nothing he likes (p. 439), illustrates the way experience is formless until the individual gives it form. In its neutrality, Howells' complicity of experience resembles what William James called "pure experience." That is, pure experience is the flux of things as yet unformed. In James's words, it is "a *that* which is not yet any definite *what*, tho' ready to be all sorts of whats." [4] In the complicity of Howells' novel there is no hard and fast line between circumstance and character, between private and public experience. In the broadest sense, the conflicts in the novel stem from different and opposing claims to know what form experience ought to take to realize justice, both for the individual and for society. If the novel does not resolve the problems it raises, its complicity nonetheless reveals a willingness to let all things grow together, and where there are conflicts of interest, to conserve as many interests as possible in accordance with something like the "economy of pain" formula announced by Sewell in *The Rise of Silas Lapham*.[5] Thus, we may say that, in a real sense, complicity in Howells' novel is an aesthetic form of the novelist's socialism.

Toward the last, March, speculating on the meaning of the death of Conrad Dryfoos, says to his wife: " 'I don't know what it all means, Isabel, though I believe it means good' " (p. 541). March's statment is a measure of his education in the novel, for his distinction between knowledge and belief is central to Howells' realism. In the novel it is in the characters' enactment of their beliefs that they shape their reality, and in that shaping is the pragmatic hazarding of their fortunes. March's affirmation that it all "means good," is not a superficial optimism. Rather, it is an affirmation of faith in the goodness of life in the awareness of the limits of human knowledge. What Howells' novel finally asks of us, as George Arms has said, "is awareness, an awareness not merely of society but of ourselves in society." [6]

A LONG and sometimes uneven novel, *The Quality of Mercy* is yet often powerful in its portrayal of character and its realization of experience. The story is that of John Milton Northwick of Boston and Hatboro, treasurer of the Ponkwasset Mills. Epitome of success and respectability in the eyes of Hatboro, Northwick is found out to be a defaulter. He is caught speculating with company funds and has juggled the books to conceal his "irregularity." Unable and unwilling to believe himself a thief, Northwick skips to Canada, leaving his two daughters in ignorance of his situation. He lets it appear that he is going to the mills on business. A day or so later a newspaper account of a railroad accident on the Canada line lists a T. W. Northwick as having apparently been a passenger aboard the wrecked train. Whether John Milton Northwick is dead becomes the question in Hatboro. At the same time Northwick's trouble with the Ponkwasset corporation is made public and adds scandal to the mystery. Northwick's daughters believe their father to have been innocent and, after a time, accept the idea that he is dead. Parts two and three of the novel flash back and forth between Northwick's existence in exile and the life in Hatboro. At the end Northwick gives himself up and dies on his return trip home to the United States.

In the synopsis of his story which he sent to his publisher, McClure, Howells described Northwick as "a man of great force, great apparent wealth and high social standing, who had worked himself up from a simple New England beginnings. . . ."[1] In his excellent discussion of the novel, Edwin Cady observes that in it Howells "was working out one of the variations on the theme of *The Rise of Silas Lapham*."[2] Lapham was also a man of great force. Unlike Northwick, however, Lapham's force was a self-confidence that drew the world into itself. Northwick's force spends itself outward into the external forms of life. Both men are selfish in different ways. Northwick lives for the appearances of life, taking pride in his "wooden palace" of a house. On the night he is preparing to skip, Northwick looks from his window at the spread of land and buildings which represent his estate: "In the silent moonlight Northwick looked at it as if it were an expansion or extension of himself, so personally did it seem to represent his tastes, and so historical was it of the ambitions of his whole life; he realized that it would be like literally tearing himself from it, when he should leave it."[3] Northwick's act of "tearing himself" away enriches the sense of the description of him as a man of "great force." For Northwick's life from now on becomes a force of will and intention in conflict with actuality. His life seems a living death. Howells' psychological study of Northwick's conflict is powerful and moving.

Northwick's situation mirrors a duality and ambiguity which are variously reflected throughout the story. The external forms of existence left behind in Hatboro shape themselves inwardly in Northwick as feverish desires and homesick dreams. Inner and outer life conflict in Northwick until it seems he must go insane. In Canada Northwick grows a beard and buys different clothes to disguise himself. The Hatboroian "respectability" nowhere shows itself; rather, it is deeply ingrained within Northwick. That Northwick's respectability is perhaps an inherited trait complicates its meaning: "He had been respectable ever since he was born; if he was born with any instinct it was the instinct of respectability, the wish to be honored for what he seemed. It was all the stronger in him, because his father had never had it; perhaps an heredi- tary trait found expression in him after passing over one generation; perhaps an antenatal influence formed him to that type" (p. 14). Northwick has come to doubt that there is a "moral government of the universe." His experience has been that good acts are not always rewarded nor bad ones punished. In- deed, bad acts are often not found out at all. Always intending to do right, "so as to be on the safe side," Northwick has been able to "compromise with his principles and to do wrong provisionally and then repair the wrong before he was found out, or before the overruling power noticed him" (pp. 29–30). As he had juggled the account books, Northwick juggles his accounting of himself. That he should imagine there is a "safe side" to be on is central to the ironic ambi- guity of his situation and to the meaning of the novel.

The railroad accident in which Northwick is pre- sumed killed causes speculation and suffering of differ- ent kinds in Hatboro and illustrates, as both Edwin Cady and Arnold Fox have observed, Howells' doc- trine of complicity.[4] In addition, the incident func- tions to point the ambiguity and uncertainty in which all are involved. Northwick's railroad "accident," for example, may be linked with the fact that his troubles began for him in his speculation in railroad stock. "In the early days of his connection with the company, it largely owed its prosperity to his wise and careful management; one might say that it was not until the last, when he got so badly caught by that drop in railroads, that he had felt anything wrong in his convertible use of its money" (pp. 11–12). Believed killed on his outward journey to Canada, Northwick actually dies on his return to the United States. The polarity of Northwick's existence is brought out in other ways. His house in Hatboro, for example, seemed almost tropical: "When the door was opened to Northwick, a pleasant heat gushed out, together with the perfume of flowers . . ." (p. 5): "Under the conservatories, with their long stretches of glass, catching the moon's rays like levels of water, was the steam furnace that imparted their summer climate, through heavy mains carried below the basement, to every chamber of the mansion . . ." (p. 19). Canada, as the frozen north of Northwick's exile, stands in another way for his divided life. Edwin Cady writes: "Cold becomes the symbol of Northwick's sin. As in many another work of literature, the no-color whiteness of the snow is an omen of evil. In letting Northwick skip away, fiery old Mr. Hilary calls him 'you whited sepulchre,' and as Northwick retreats into the bush he is ever more deeply oppressed by the 'lifeless desert he had been travelling through.' "[5] Northwick's dead wife, whom he had so often to "push" out of his thoughts because of her "troublesome solicitudes and her entire uselessness in important matters," had kept her parlor in Northwick's house on its south side: "It faced southward behind the house to the bulk of woods." Living to himself, Northwick had excluded his wife. The flight to Canada continues his exclusion of others from his life; but, ironically, Northwick now intends to make restitution "to those he had injured" by means of the money he has won in speculation with company funds. It is this intention which becomes his "will"; and, "though he might seem a defaulter, he was a man with a sacred trust, and a high purpose" (p. 220). The man who had wanted to be honored for what he seemed, now believes he is to be honored for what he intends. His children's name must be cleared; his creditors must not suffer loss; he must "rehabilitate" himself. To achieve these ends Northwick is "careful of his life and health." He must not, he tells himself, "die."

After having wired ahead for a chair on the Montreal Pullman, Northwick decides instead to go directly to Quebec. That will be faster and safer. Though he laughs to himself in thinking how he has "baffled fate," he also had "bargained with God that if He would let him escape," he would do all in his power to make it up to his creditors. By virtue of "this understanding with Providence," Northwick imagines he will be able to elude any police who may be waiting for him along the way. God's authority is appealed to against society's law. Journeying ever northward into himself and away from the world, Northwick becomes increasingly aware of a duality in his life, of a struggle for supremacy between his "will" and his "mind." All his will is bent to make him live outwardly in the present in Canada, but his mind keeps drawing him back to Hatboro. In a moment of seeming strength and calmness of purpose, just before entry to Canada, Northwick takes account of himself:

> At Stanstead he ceased altogether to deal with the past in his thoughts. He was now safe from it beyond any possible peradventure, and he began to plan for the future. . . . His mind worked nimbly and docilely now, with none of that perversity which had troubled him during the day with the fear that he was going wrong in it. His thought was clear and quick, and it obeyed his will like a part of it; that sense of duality in himself no longer agonized him. He took a calm and

prudent survey of the work before him; and he saw how essential it was that he should make no false step. . . . (p. 219)

Arrived in Quebec, Northwick, to hide his identity as an American, dresses as the Canadians do. His "hard" American hat he replaces with a "soft" one of fur. His winter journey, oddly, recalls to Northwick a summer one made years ago with his wife. Reality seems to slip out of all focus in Northwick's waking-sleep. Stopping at one place to rest, Northwick sleeps and dreams— "of himself . . . People were talking of him, and one said how old he was; and another looked at his long, white beard which flowed down over the blanket as far as his waist . . . he showed them how he could take it off and put it on at pleasure. He started awake. . . ." (pp. 239–40). On his return from Canada, Northwick falls into a seeming sleep on the train and dies. With the full revolution of his life's journey done, Northwick comes to his final home in the death which ends the conflict in his life.

Going from Quebec to St. Anne's, to St. Joachim, to Baie St. Paul, past "the great Capes Trinity and Eternity," Northwick comes to "Haha Bay," named for its effect of giving an echo. Past echoes to present in Northwick. The cabin he stops at he recognizes as the one he and his wife had stopped at that long ago summer; the same man, too, still keeps the cabin. Northwick remembers how his wife had liked the man and had told him that she "would like to live in such a house in such a place, and should not be afraid of the winter that he told her was so terrible" (p. 242). Inside the cabin it seems to Northwick that the "room and the furniture in it were absolutely unchanged." A chair there is the one his wife used to sit in to look out on the garden—as she had done in Hatboro—behind the house. "But for the frost on the pane," Northwick

believes he could see the garden and the things growing there even now. When Mr. Bird, the owner of the
cabin, tries to find out why Northwick is in Canada,
the latter forces himself "to get his mind to grapple
with his real motive . . . his mind kept pulling away
from him, like that unruly horse, and he could not
manage it" (p. 246). The "unruly horse" subtly recalls the opening scene of the novel where, having
been met at the train by his man and the cutter,
Northwick has a near accident on his way home:

> . . . the little slender black figure of a man that started
> up in the middle of the road, as if it had risen out of the
> ground, had an even vivid distinctness. He must have
> been lying in the snow; the horses crouched back with a
> sudden recoil, as if he had struck them back with his
> arm, and plunged the runners of the cutter into the
> deeper snow beside the beaten track. He made a slight
> pause, long enough to give Northwick a contemptuous
> glance, and then continued along the road at a leisurely
> pace to the deep cut through the snow from the next
> house. Here he stood regarding such difficulty as North-
> wick had in quieting his horses, and getting underway
> again. (p. 4)

Thirty-six pages later we learn who the man was
Northwick had almost run down. " 'It was the *Law*
you tried to drive over!' " exclaims lawyer Putney.
    The law Northwick almost runs down with his
"force"—symbolized in the power of his horses—
should be understood as law in the broadest sense.
We remember Northwick had called on God to keep
him safe from the police; and, at the end of the novel,
Putney, who has become legal consultant for Northwick's daughters, tells Dr. Morrell that he is not sorry
that Northwick, at the last, "slipped through" the
fingers of justice. Northwick would not have made a
good example anyway. He was, in Putney's eyes, only

" 'a kind of—incident; and a pretty common kind. He was a mere creature of circumstances—like the rest of us! His environment made him rich, and his environment made him a rogue. Sometimes I think there *was* nothing to Northwick, except what happened to him' " (p. 474). Putney's reasoning suggests some fatal law operative in circumstances, with Northwick as victim. Putney wonders what Morrell thinks of " 'a world where we fellows keep fuming and fizzing away, with our little aims and purposes, and the great ball of life seems to roll calmly along, and get where it's going without the slightest reference to what we do or don't do?' " He guesses that it may be " 'all Fate.' " Morrell guesses, though, that it may be " 'Law.' " Putney then says, optimistically: " 'taking it by and large, and seeing that most things seem to turn out pretty well in the end, I'll split the difference with you and call it Mercy.' "

Northwick's "pretty common kind" of history is the realist's study of the commonplace with all its inscrutability. Is it the voice of some transcendent law that speaks to Northwick of his innocence? Is his character his fate? These are alternative possibilities of meaning. No single idea, however, can satisfactorily explain the significance of Northwick's history.

At Haha Bay, with the breaking up of winter and of a fever which has left him weak, Northwick makes a gesture toward spiritual recovery by writing a letter to the Boston *Events*, asking for a chance to make such restitution as he can. The appearance of the letter in the paper is the first sign to Hatboro that Northwick is still alive, and it causes various reactions there. Eben Hilary, President of the Board of the mills, who had urged that Northwick be given three day's grace to prove himself an honest man when his "irregularity" had been discovered, is relieved—especially since, in anger, he had told Northwick that " 'the best thing that could happen to you . . . would be a good railroad accident' " (p. 10). Hilary, ironically, is glad to be free "from the oppressive sense of responsibility" for Northwick's death. William Gerrish, a leading business man, expresses no faith in Northwick's declaration of good intentions: " 'when he makes the first payment to his creditors—I will believe that he is sorry for what he has done, and not *till* then.' " Joyed to learn that their father is alive, Adeline and Suzette Northwick are stunned to think that he could ever have been dishonest. Adeline believes her father is "crazy" and explains his confession in this light. She had imagined that her father would come back to life and show Hatboro that it had believed a lie about him; but now it seems to her as if he " 'had broken his word to *us*. That is what kills me.' " In a word broken and a law broken, Howells' tragicomic ironies proliferate. Sue insists, though there is no legal need for it, that she and her sister must give up the Northwick property to the creditors. " 'How do we know that father had any right to give it to us when he did?' " she demands. Her father having shown himself to be dishonest, Sue can "never" forgive him; " 'He is dead to me, *now!*' " (p. 286). Death, in the various guises which it assumes in Howells' novel, seems usually to stand for false self-assertion.

Alonzo Pinney, formerly a reporter for the *Events* and a sometime detective, but always one with a nose for the facts, is hired by Eben Hilary's socialistically-minded and well-meaning son, Matt, to go to Canada to find Northwick. The idea originally is Pinney's, for he had thought it would make a good story to offer to the *Events*. Because incidents involving defaulters have become "commonplace," however, the *Events* gives Pinney no encouragement. Pinney, urged by

Matt Hilary, decides instead to seek Northwick in the interests of his family. In addition, Pinney tells his wife that he plans to go in his capacity as a detective and, thus, collect the reward offered for Northwick. Mrs. Pinney declares this would be dishonest. " 'Don't you try to carry water on both shoulders,' " she warns her husband. Her warning echoes the earlier confession of Eben Hilary to Matt when the latter tells his father that he and Sue Northwick are going to be married. Hilary takes it well but says he will have to resign from the Board. As its president he is *"ex-officio,"* Northwick's enemy. To continue in that position with Matt married to Sue would not be quite right. Futhermore, he has entertained a secret hope that Northwick might "escape the consequences of his crime," and the Board has suspected this senti-ment in him. " 'I *have* tried to carry water on both shoulders,' " he says to Matt. A short time after, Mrs. Hilary, trying to make her daughter see that she is socially superior to the talented but inferior young writer Brice Maxwell, and warning her to steer clear of love for him because it could never work where two people are so different in their backgrounds, says: " 'You must understand . . . and understand dis-tinctly, that you can't live on two levels; the world won't let you' " (pp. 386–87). Northwick does live on two levels, though, in the dualistic conflict between his inner and outer lives, between his past and present, between his intentions and the facts. Harmony is re-stored for Northwick only as he comes to grant the validity of both inner and outer existence as making up his life. Both have their different claims, and some adjustment must be made between them. Mrs. Hilary is right in seeing that a person's life must be one thing; but it is one only insofar as it is experienced as one. In a continually changing multiplicity of experience, however, man's inner and outer selves must make pragmatic shift to get along. Unable in the conflicting dualism of his situation to establish a satisfactory correspondence between intention and actuality, Northwick becomes almost insane.

In his role as friend to Northwick and Northwick's family, Pinney does well, though the newspaper man in him shows through at times. Remembering his wife's advice that he must be one thing, however, he rises to his occasion and even grows fond of Northwick, whom he sometimes regards as being like his own "father," especially when Northwick asks Pinney to handcuff him. Pinney promises that he will see to it that there will be no "interviewing" and no reporters at the trial if Northwick will come back—though near the end of the novel Putney remarks that Pinney " 'considers himself a ruined man; he's left off detecting for a living, and gone back to interviewing.' "

Before his final return with Pinney, Northwick steals back to Hatboro and his house—"he must steal into his house as he has stolen out of it"—for a secret visit. The house, stripped now of all the things which had meant home in Northwick's earlier life, shows a "desolation" of "dismantled and abandoned rooms" (p. 428). Lighting his way with a taper match, Northwick is like "a ghost come back in search of his body." A window mirror—to look out is to see in—shows in the shadow-light Northwick in his costume of long white hair and beard: "His own childern would not have known him." Reminiscent of Shakesperian theatre in its atmosphere—Northwick had been to see *Macbeth* and afterward found "it was all true"—, the scene is a powerful evocation of the sense of loss in a mind baffled by the ghosts of reality.

Returning to Canada and summoning Pinney at last to come take him back to the United States,

Northwick is aware of there being mixed with his longing for home "a desire, feeble and formless enough, for expiation. There began to be suggested to him from somewhere, somehow, something like the thought that if he really had done wrong, there might be rest and help in accepting the legal penalty, disproportionate and excessive as it might be" (p. 464). Northwick summons Pinney not out of any altruistic motive to help advance the latter's career as budding detective, but because he dreads "the long journey alone; he wanted the comfort of Pinney's society . . . he instinctively desired the kindly, lying sympathy of a soul that had so much affinity with his own" (p. 464). Northwick's "long journey alone" approaches its end in his acceptance of society's claim on him and in his recognition that that claim is as valid as his own purposes and beliefs in the complicity of existence. Society now, rather than Northwick, will claim the whole man as its own in *its* imperfect justice. Pinney tells Northwick: " 'It's going to cost you something. It's going to cost you all you've brought with you . . . and more' " (p. 416).

Eben Hilary had once jokingly remarked that Northwick was " 'one of our *least* remarkable men' "; and we recall that Putney had confided to Dr. Morrell that Northwick seemed " 'to be a kind of incident; and a pretty common kind.' " Stealing from one side of his life for the sake of the other, Northwick is one more commonplace character in Howells' gallery of realistic portraits. Mrs. Hilary had warned her daughter that the world wouldn't let her live on two levels. " 'Either you must be in the world and of it entirely; or you must discard its criterions, and form your own, and hover about in a sort of Bohemian limbo on its outskirts; or you must give it up altogether' " (p. 387). This, in sum, is Northwick's history. Living at first for the world at expense of self, he then sought to live for self at the expense of the world; finally, he lost his life altogether in death on the return home.

Howells' imaginative grasp of man's division and unity in life is a constant theme throughout his fiction. Accepting both division and unity as the reality of the human situation—pragmatism, said William James, equally abjures "absolute monism and absolute pluralism" [6]—Howells rejected either "side" as standing for the whole of experience: psychological, social, metaphysical. These categories of experience, of course, overlap in the concrete, dramatic experience of art in the novels. For convenience we may say that in fiction Howells presents existence in its micro-macrocosmic guise. It should be understood, however, that particular and universal are interactive in Howells' pragmatism. Reality in his fiction is not static nor held in abstraction from experience; rather, reality is emergent out of conflict.

Unable in his situation to know existence as wholly one or many, man struggles toward unity. The world, to quote William James again, "is growing more and more unified by those systems of connexion at least which human energy keeps framing as time goes on." [7] In *The Quality of Mercy* jurisprudence is one of those systems man makes to mediate as best he can between the conflict of the one and the many. That there also exists somehow, somewhere, some other Jurisprudence as an ultimate system beyond all experience is knowledge man does not certainly have. Putney, for example, guesses at Fate as an ultimate principle operative in human life; Morrell guesses at Law. Northwick himself, we recall, had called on Divine Providence. Assertions that existence is finally one are problematic in experience. Man's law and justice, Howells shows, are necessarily imperfect, as is man's knowledge. If the

Board of Directors of the Ponkwasset Mills does not get its pound of flesh from Northwick, it is, as Putney hints at the last, mercy for Northwick as well as for society.

THE LANDLORD AT LION'S HEAD, one of Howells' lesser-
known but better novels, opens with a depiction of
Lion's Head Mountain that foreshadows the novelist's
manipulation of point of view in the story. In viewing
the mountain, one grows aware of an ambiguous quality about it: "If you looked at the mountain from the
west, the line of the summit was wandering and uncertain, like that of most mountain-tops; but, seen from
the east, the mass of granite showing above the dense
forests of the lower slopes had the form of a sleeping
lion." [1] What one sees is apparently determined by
one's point of view. The lion's body, seen from the
east, is only vaguely discernible; but its head is "boldly
sculptured against the sky" in a likeness that could
not be more perfect "if it had been a definite intention or art." Often hidden by clouds in winter, Lion's
Head, in summer, "was a part of the landscape, as
imperative and importunate as the Great Stone Face
itself" (p. 3).

Howells here is almost certainly alluding to Hawthorne's story, "The Great Stone Face." The mountain
in that story comes to stand for an image of faith in
divinity. In Howells' novel the mountain is that which
is given the world as fact, standing imperatively over
us and against us while importuning us to make some-

thing of it. What the people in the novel do make of
the mountain and, by analogy, of its hero, Jeff Durgin,
is what Howells' story is about. Edwin Cady observes
that "the problem of the novel is to see what it will
mean that Jeff becomes the landlord at Lion's Head." [2]
Reading the novel as a Howellsian "research into the
plight of civilization in modern American life," Cady,
while recognizing that Howells does not tell us what
to think, tends to conclude that Jeff, "for all his com-
pensating attractiveness, is a bully, a 'blackguard,' and
a savage—completely beyond the reach of discipline
from within or without." George N. Bennett, on the
other hand, declares that Howells "was not interested
in merely *showing* Jeff; he wanted to *understand* him.
As much as he disapproved of him, Howells did not
fall into the easy simplification of portraying a blackguard." Noting Jeff Durgin's lack of moral sense,
Bennett concludes that he is one more Howells "reminder that anything less than the highest conception
of the individual responsibility is bound to result in a
corresponding reduction of moral accomplishment." [3]
Doubtless the majority of us are more at ease with the
Westovers—the Boston artist in the story—than with
the Jeff Durgins of the world. Knowing well the challenge the Jeff Durgins make to our inmost selves,
Howells, apologizing to C. E. Norton for the "unpleasant" people in his story said, not without irony: "The
pleasant people *are* more familiar to our experience;
you are entirely right; and I do not know why I should
have made so many unpleasant ones, unless it is because they are easier to do." [4] To see what it would
mean that Jeff Durgin became the landlord at Lion's
Head, Howells knew, would be to see what it meant
to some of his pleasant people.

Since Howells' novel draws a parallel between life
and art, it is fitting that, as Cady also notes, we see Jeff

Durgin mainly through the eyes of the Boston artist, Jere Westover. As the story begins, Westover, hiking one summer's day through primitive up-country New England, finds himself arrived at an isolated farmhouse. Introducing himself to the people there, he explains that he has come to paint Lion's Head Mountain. If Mrs. Durgin will let him stay on for a few days while he works at his painting, Westover will pay for his food and lodging; thus, ironically, Westover is instrumental in that process which eventually leads to Durgin's farm becoming a fancy summer hotel that is repugnant to Westover. The artist stays longer than he had thought at first would be necessary: his portrait of the mountain keeps coming out not just right. Through the years, however, he keeps trying to get it right.

Struggling one afternoon to get his picture right in a changing afternoon light, but succeeding only in getting his canvas "into such a state that he alone could have found it much more intelligible than his palette," Westover is interrupted by young Jeff Durgin intently looking on over the artist's shoulder. Jeff complains that he doesn't think Westover's picture of the mountain "looks very much like it." Amused and flattered by this, as he takes it, "popular censure" speaking in Jeff, Westover condescendingly suggests that perhaps Jeff doesn't know about such things. When Jeff stubbornly replies, " 'I know what I see,' " Westover answers that he doubts it (p. 19). The incident not only establishes a significant difference in point of view between Westover and Jeff that is complexly developed throughout the novel, it serves to alert us to larger aesthetic and moral issues in Howells' novel. Whether it be Lion's Head or Jeff Durgin, what is made of them is intimately related to the person who is the maker—the "artist." In the novel

the subject-object relationship is interactive, constitu-
ting a complicity of experience in which the subject-
object reality is emergent. The success of Westover's
repeated attempts to get Lion's Head right is directly
dependent on the view of the mountain—and Jeff—
which he takes.

By depicting Jeff Durgin from different points of
view, and by demonstrating that the act of seeing and
judging is relative to the person who sees, Howells
suggests that no perception of Jeff may represent all
views. Westover's pressing Jeff to accept full responsibility for his actions is a position of limited value by
reason of Jeff's mixed conditionality as shown in the
story. As opposed to Westover's view of Jeff, however,
another possible one is advanced by Mr. Whitwell, a
neighbor of the Durgins. A philosopher of sorts, Yan-
kee style, Whitwell has a quizzical and sharp intelli-
gence which has the effect of whittling Westover's
sober moralizing about Jeff down to a more human
size. Talking with Westover about Jeff's teasing of
little Cynthia Whitwell, for example, Whitwell says:
" 'I don't suppose a fellow's so much to blame, if he's
got the devil in him, as what the devil is.' " Westover,
already showing a temperamental aversion for Jeff and
an attraction to Cynthia, whom he is ready to marry
in the end, tends to feel that Jeff's teasing is "original
sin" with Jeff himself. Whitwell guesses that it is not
original sin, though: Jeff's maternal grandfather, a
scoundrel who had kept a tavern over on the west side
of Lion's Head, had always been on the "mean side"
of any question. Whitwell's more liberal and open
view as opposed to Westover's more conservative one
is also demonstrated in regard to the artist's portrait of
Lion's Head Mountain. When neighbors come to
watch the artist at work—and Jeff's pleasure at playing
host to them points toward his emergence in the end

as the landlord at Lion's Head Hotel—there is no question in their minds but one of "likeness; all finer facts were far from them; they wished to see how good a portrait Westover had made, and some of them consoled him with the suggestion that the likeness would come out more when the picture got dry" (p. 36). Whitwell, acting in his characteristically generous way, attempts "a larger view of the artist's work," suggesting to Westover that " 'you could not always get a thing like that just right the first time, and that you had to keep trying till you did get it; but it paid in the end' " (p. 36). Howells, we note, speaks in the preface to the Library Edition of his novel of trying to "get" his story, feeling that it did pay in the end (p. viii).

Five years pass and Westover, returning from study in France, where things are being done right, is disappointed to find the Durgin farm changed into a hotel for summer people. The changes strike him as being "tasteless and characterless . . . There was a vulgar modernity in the new parts." Going into Mrs. Durgin, Westover asks for his old room. When she wonders whether he might not like something a little nicer, Westover replies: " 'I don't believe you've got anything nicer.' " And the Boston artist gets his old room with the old view of Lion's Head!

Westover finds Jeff now grown into a young man. His "stalwart frame . . . notable for strength rather than height," clearly links Jeff here with the primitive and the powerful as they are suggested by Lion's Head Mountain. Mrs. Durgin, who is ambitious for her son to be more than a tavern keeper, wants him to study law at Harvard. She proudly tells Westover that at the academy Jeff has kept up with Cynthia Whitwell. In the relationship between Jeff and Cynthia, Howells reveals a psychological basis for point of view. The eventual break between Jeff and Cynthia, for instance, climaxes a pattern of relationship between them which is initiated early in the novel: then, young Jeff once threw apples at little Cynthia, and she ran for cover into the schoolhouse; another time, when Jeff frightened Cynthia with his dog, she threatened to tell teacher on him. Now, at "Lovewell" academy, Jeff struggles to keep up with Cynthia but dislikes school strongly. Later, Cynthia will insist that Jeff finish at Harvard before they marry. Finally, after their break, Cynthia herself becomes a Boston schoolteacher. In the story Cynthia and Westover are both on the side of law and order and civilization. Jeff, though, is an opposing force. At Harvard and in Boston, the powerful country boy—"his yeomanly vigor and force," Westover reflects, "threaten the more worldly conceptions of the tailor with danger"—is regarded as a "jay," an outsider. At a tea for the Vostrands in his Boston studio, Westover is asked by one lady: Who " 'was your friend who ought to have worn a lionskin and carried a club?' " (p. 115).

Jeff's affair of sorts with the bored Boston socialite, Bessie Lynde—" 'He's a riddle, and I'm all the time guessing at him,' " she remarks to a girl friend,—precipitates his break with Cynthia. Though Westover, shocked that Jeff isn't "able to see" the wrongness of his actions, insists that it is Jeff's duty to break off with Cynthia, the causes of that break as it happens in the story are more complex than Westover is able to see. Another time, when Bessie Lynde's alcoholic brother, Alan, gets drunk at a party with Jeff in attendance, Westover blames Jeff for it. Jeff argues that it may be so from Westover's " 'point of view,' " which assumes " 'that everything is done from a purpose, or that a thing is intended because it's done.' " As Jeff sees it, " 'most things in this world are not thought about, and not intended. They happen, just as much as the other things that we call accidents' " (p. 248). Later, when Whitwell asks whether Jeff has been up to "any deviltry" lately, Westover says, " 'Nothing that I can call intentional.' " Whitwell wants to know, though, what Jeff has *done*. After Westover tells him about the Alan Lynde incident, Whitwell, satisfied that Jeff had held no grudge against Lynde, tentatively concludes that " 'it might have been an accident' " (pp. 264–65). Which theory about the facts in Jeff's history best explains that history is the problem of the novel. One theory may explain it more satisfactorily than another; but, as William James noted, "that means more satisfactorily to ourselves, and individuals will emphasize their points of satisfaction differently." [5]

Jeff's meaning is both single and multiple in contexts that are particular and accumulative in the novel. For example, when he takes Bessie Lynde in his arms and kisses her, Jeff, in his crude strength, may be seen in terms of sexual energy; but in that Jeff is linked with Lion's Head Mountain, his energy suggests some kind of ultimate life-force in Nature. Or, where Jeff's full name is Thomas Jefferson Durgin, his energy may be taken to represent a thrust toward freedom over against the conventions of Harvard and Boston and society generally. Standing for a social form exhausted by its own rigidity, Bessie Lynde is incapable of containing Jeff's "power," his need to shape himself in the given world. Fulfillment for Jeff comes in his union with Genevieve Vostrand, whose forced marriage with a member of an effete aristocratic Italian family failed, though she bore a child in that union. Paralleling this development in Jeff's life is his emergence as the successful landlord at Lion's Head Hotel, a building, Whitwell admiringly notes to a disapproving Westover, styled in the manner of the Renaissance.

Howells conceived life as a complicity of self and other, an organic inclusiveness in which self and other interacted to create a various reality in a changing and continuing experience. A version of this idea is given by Jeff late in the novel.

> Life had, so far, not been what he meant it, and just now it occurred to him that he might not have wholly made it what it had been. It seemed to him that a good many other people had come in and taken a hand in making his own life what it had been; and if he had meddled with theirs more than he was wanted, it was about an even thing. As far as he could make out, he was a sort of ingredient in the general mixture. He had probably done his share of the flavoring, but he had had very little to do with the mixing. There were different ways of looking at the thing. Westover had his way, but it struck Jeff that it put too much responsibility on the ingredient, and too little on the power that chose it. He believed that he could prove a clear case in his own favor, as far as the question of final justice was concerned, but he had no complaints to make. Things had fallen out very much to his mind. He was the Landlord at Lion's Head, at last. . . . (p. 364)

Jeff comes into his own at the last, but that it is *his* own, as Westover urges, is shown as problematic in the novel. Near the end, Westover, Jeremiah-like, prophesies that, according to the certain moral government in things, Jeff Durgin "will reap what he has sown." The problem is to know just what Jeff has sown. Whitwell inclines to think that Jeff may be a better man than he was a boy, that he may have changed in heart. As evidence for this possibility, he recalls how Jeff, still smarting from a whip lashing

once administered him by Alan Lynde, afterward gave
up vengeance on Lynde in a moment of rage to kill
him. As Jeff himself remembered it later, his mercy
toward Lynde then was a "mystery he did not try to
solve." Relenting a little, Westover concedes that perhaps " 'we're all broken shafts, here.' " After all, he
continues, there may be something in that " 'old hypothesis of another life, a world where there is room
enough and time enough for all the beginnings of this
to complete themselves—' " (p. 400).

So far as the question of final justice is concerned,
Jeff feels that he could prove a "clear" case for himself; and where it is a question of final justice, he may
be right. The complicity of his situation as depicted in
Howells' novel, however, admits of no "clear" case
either for or against Jeff, Westover notwithstanding.
Essentially conservative, one who cherishes the old order, Westover is sensitive to all that threatens life's conventional decencies as he sees them. "He was an artist,
and he had always been a bohemian, but at heart he
was philistine and bourgeois. His ideal was a settle-
ment, a fixed habitation, a stated existence, a home
where he could work constantly in an air of affection,
and unselfishly do his part to make his home happy"
(p. 402). It is not surprising in the end, though the
mystery of it remains, that Westover rather than Jeff
gets Cynthia Whitwell, "the pure and lovely Puritan
maid," as Edwin Cady calls her. It may be said that
Cynthia's portrait, which Westover paints, turns out to
be his real picture of Lion's Head; for what his experience has come to mean for him is the discovery of his
love for Cynthia.

Whitwell's "larger view" of Jeff balances Westover's more closed one and keeps intact Howells'
attempt to get *his* picture of Jeff Durgin in the fullness of his mixed reality. Showing Jeff's reality and

that of the other characters in his novel as mixed and made by the characters themselves in their experience, Howells reveals himself as an artist who does not attempt to justify his characters or to pass judgment on them. In this sense his novel is not simply one which deals with changing social and moral conditions in Howells' America. Jeff's story may be seen in terms of conflicting moral values in a changing society; or, as a conflict between primitive and civilized man; or, as a conflict between West and East in American culture. These things are there; but, they are there for Howells as Lion's Head is there for Westover: they are the materials out of which the artist makes his art. And to Howells the art of making art meant being true to life, true to the lives his characters made in their fictional experience. In this pragmatic realism there could be no finished portrait of Jeff Durgin. He had to remain both realized and unrealized. Indeed, this was the condition of his "reality."

Writing about Howells' novel, Oscar Firkins interestingly observed: "The story . . . is comparatively rich in effective incident, though when, after emergence from the final exit, you turn back to survey the edifice, the edifice has vanished. There is cohesion, but there is no perspective." [6] I think Firkins unconsciously pays tribute to Howells' artistry in manipulating point of view to create the Mountain that is and is not there and which remains a riddle "as imperative and importunate as the Great Stone Face itself." In Hawthorne's story, Ernest all his life looks for the man born in the image of the Great Stone Face, an image of the divine. Before we learn that Ernest is himself that man by reason of his faith, he thinks to have found him in a poet whose works he has come to love. When the poet denies it, Ernest queries whether the thoughts in his poetry are not divine.

"They have a strain of divinity," replied the poet. "You can hear in them the far-off echo of a heavenly song. But my life, dear Ernest, has not corresponded with my thoughts. I have had grand dreams, but they have been only dreams, because I have lived—and that, too, by my own choice—among poor and mean realities."

In *The Landlord at Lion's Head*, Howells says no more, and no less, than the poet.

IN *The Son of Royal Langbrith*, Howells explores a
subject that fascinated Hawthorne, the influence of
the past on the present. How the shadow of the dead
Royal Langbrith falls on the living and shapes their
lives is the central situation of the novel. Young James
Langbrith idealizes his dead father, ignorant of the
fact that his father had led a "double" life. A model in
public life of the good man and citizen, Royal Langbrith in his private life had been brutal and selfish.
Knowledge about the private life of the dead man is
limited to his widow, to Dr. Anther—who desires to
marry Mrs. Langbrith—and to John Langbrith,
brother of the deceased and now manager of the
Langbrith paper mill in Saxmills, Massachusetts.
Others who come to know Royal Langbrith's hidden
history include Judge Garley, the Reverend Mr.
Enderby, and Mr. Hawberk. Driven out of the mill
business by Royal Langbrith after having helped to
make the business a success with an invention of his,
Hawberk took to using opium and became an addict.
His effort to regain health and sanity is a key element
in the novel's exploration of its subject.

In Royal Langbrith's "double" life, Howells again
recognizes a dualism in experience that is depicted
variously in the novel. Dr. Anther, for example, strives

to make Mrs. Langbrith his wife, but circumstances prevent their marriage. George N. Bennett has put it succinctly: "Mrs. Langbrith would marry Dr. Anther but for the fact of her son's idolatry of his father. To marry without telling him would destroy his faith in her; to tell would destroy his image of his father." [1] Anther must deal not only with his own will but with circumstances as well. Mrs. Langbrith, on the other hand, seems a victim of circumstances. She has been unable to make herself tell her son about his father, which Anther regards as a lack of will on her part. For Mrs. Langbrith, though, it has been easier not to tell James, easier to let be the illusion about the man that is the image which James worships. In his fondness for the signs of place and power, James seems shallow. Yet, he is proud of his family's old royalty. James on one occasion tells his friend from Harvard that the Langbrith family name had once been " 'Longueha-leine, and they translated it after they came to England into Longbreath, or Langbrith, as we have it. I believe I prefer our final form. It's splendidly suggestive for a bookplate. . . .' " [2] At dinner, James shows "a baronial preference" in carving the turkey. "He fancied an old-fashioned, old-family effect from it." James's faith in the appearances of things is pointed in his fascination at the face of his father in a painting of Royal Langbrith which had been copied from a photograph. James says to Falk, his Harvard friend: " 'Those old New England faces . . . have a great charm. From a child, that face of my father's fascinated me. As I got on, and began to be interested in my environment, I read into it all I had read out of Hawthorne about the Puritan type. I put the grim old chaps out of *The Scarlet Letter* and *The House of the Seven Gables* and the *Twice-Told Tales* into it, and interpreted my father by them. But, really, I knew very little about him' " (pp. 25–26).

Edwin H. Cady has remarked that "in the father-image of the son of Royal Langbrith, Justin Anther discovers the most Hawthorne-like of all the moral tensions in Howells' novels. The mysteries of how the evil men do lives after them are, in fact, no more profoundly explored anywhere in Hawthorne than here."[3] Both Howells and Hawthorne explored inner and outer experience in their depiction of the nature of reality. Unlike the romancer, however, Howells looked steadily into the ordinary and probable rather than away from them, finding his mysteries in facts. In the progress of the novel, James Langbrith gains a fuller perception of his father and, accepting his new knowledge, learns to live with it.

James's announcement that he intends to present to the Saxmills library a memorial plaque bearing his father's likeness is a turning point in the novel. Anther's failure to respond enthusiastically to the idea when James first proposes it leads James to ask Judge Garley and the Reverend Mr. Enderby to officiate at the dedication ceremony. Anther, meanwhile, feels it his duty to tell Garley and Enderby what he knows about Royal Langbrith. More than Garley, Enderby is sensitive to the moral intricacies posed by the situation. Both he and Garley, however, feel that no good can come for Saxmills by exposing Royal Langbrith, and they agree to speak at the dedication ceremony. At the urging of Mrs. Langbrith, Anther, for James's sake, attends the ceremony. He is warmly received by James, who is joyed that his father's old friend—as he believes Anther to be—has overcome his reluctance and come at the last. As he takes his seat on the platform, Anther is cheered by the crowd. Also appearing, though he has not been invited, is Hawberk. Believing that Royal Langbrith had put Hawberk out of the mill business because of his addiction to drugs, the townspeople feel Hawberk's presence is a desecration, and they greet him with cheers of derision.

Hawberk's delusion in the nightmare world of his opium dreams and his recovery from them is relevant to the dualism in experience in the novel. In his dreams, Hawberk has imagined a past in which Royal Langbrith was his good friend and a kind of "good genius." As Hawberk gradually regains his health, he begins to understand that Royal Langbrith had used him wrongly. Hawberk tells Anther: " 'Royal Langbrith seems to have a better grip as a good genius when I've been dipping into the laudanum pretty freely than he does when I've kept to the medicine and the tonics.' " Hawberk's "cure" marks his emergence into the daylight of actuality, but it should be noted that his cure is never complete. If he is freed from his opium dream of Royal Langbrith as a "good genius," there nevertheless remains the shadow of that dream to dim the clarity of Hawberk's new perception of his relationship to Langbrith. Hawberk's precarious balance of health in mind and body, the novel implies, is the precariousness of truth and reality in experience itself.

Judge Garley speaks first at the dedication ceremony, tracing the historical background of Saxmills from its earliest days. While he never knew Royal Langbrith personally, Garley says—" 'from his work I *know* him.' " Anther, we are told, laughs bitterly to himself at Garley's concluding words about Royal Langbrith: " 'Such was the man, such was the character, such was the personality whose counterfeit presentment shall be revealed to us this day, and each day shall show him to others after we are dust, as long as stone and bronze shall endure' " (p. 223). Enderby, too, appeals to the beneficial effect on Saxmills of the good deeds of Royal Langbrith, deeds that are being perpetuated in the honor shown to the memory of the father by his son. "In this he had not only testified his reverence to his father's memory, but had borne important witness to the imperishable vitality of a good deed in this world. . . . Such, in fact, was the potency of a good deed that, if done from the most selfish motive, it took no color from the motive" (p. 226). Enderby, as he speaks, has his back turned toward Anther; but the latter "had not needed the comment of the speaker's face to convey all the latent meaning" of the words to him. At the climactic moment in the proceedings—the unveiling of the plaque bearing Royal Langbrith's likeness—there is an accident. James Langbrith pulls at the cord to separate the curtains veiling the table, but "the contrivance" does not work. As James gives the cord an impatient tug, "the whole contrivance came away, dropping to the ground." The incident is a skillful reduction through humor of the solemn pretensions of the occasion. It functions, moreover, to point the futility of man's claim to truth—in this case the truth about Royal Langbrith—when his knowledge is ambiguous and imperfect.

It is on the night of the day of the ceremony, as Cady has observed, that the "salvation" of James Langbrith begins.[4] Returning home from Hope Hawberk's—they are in love and marry at the end of the novel—James surprises his mother and Anther in an embrace and learns of their love. Their act, as James sees it, is a profanation of his dead father's memory. Though he would vent his whole rage on them, James, again as Cady points out, is held in check by his own newly realized love for Hope Hawberk. The moment marks the initiation of James Langbrith, in his egoistic innocence, into the complexities of human experience in the novel.

Meanwhile, Dr. Anther, with the help of Garley and Enderby, comes to a better understanding of his own situation. Garley, however, with his legal minded habit of criticizing facts and motives, has not proven as sympathetic and understanding as Enderby, a clergyman who has "that instant self-forgetfulness natural to the born priest." In Enderby, Anther is able to feel that he deals with "a man who could appropriate his facts and realize his motives to their remotest intimations and finest significances. Science and religion met in the study of life laid bare between them" (p. 211). Anther tells Enderby what he knows about Royal Langbrith. Langbrith, says Anther, had died suddenly and "secretly" in a smoking car of a train coming up from Boston with his brother, John. Thus, the man had died "as secretly" as he had lived. Enderby thinks that no good could come now from revealing Langbrith's past: " 'We must leave it all to God now, as it has been left hitherto. He will know when the son can best bear his father's shame. He will know how to do justice, and when, on the memory of the dead; but until now, in mercy to the living, He has forborne' " (pp. 212–13). Our trust in Enderby's judgment as he expresses it here is necessarily qualified, however, by the circumstances surrounding the revelation made to James about his father. The revelation comes through John Langbrith when he meets James, who is returning from Europe, on a train coming up from Boston. John Langbrith, suffering from an attack of indigestion brought on by some cold beans and apple pie, and taking offense at "the indefinable touch of Europe" about James, flares out in vengeful and self-righteous anger against what he feels is James's patronizing air and reveals the scoundrel Royal Langbrith was. If John's is the voice of divine judgment, it speaks in "uncertain" grammar; Royal Langbrith,

John fumes, " 'ought to have went smack, smooth to hell, like shot out of a shovel!' " (p. 327). Further ambiguity is added to the comedy here when we recall that it was in just such a smoking car that Royal Langbrith died, coming up from Boston on the train with his brother.

The "curious shifting of grounds of judgment" which Anther experiences in his attitude toward James and Mrs. Langbrith is a sign of his growing recognition that his power to control circumstances is limited. When Mrs. Langbrith informs Anther that she can not go through with their marriage, he is not surprised. From his somewhat naturalistic point of view as a physician, Anther reasons that Mrs. Langbrith in her weakness represents "one of those weak forms of animal life which gather their strength for a sudden spurt, and then, when it is spent, rest helpless till their forces are renewed" (p. 265). Nor does he blame Mrs. Langbrith for being weak in dealing with her son—no more "than he would have blamed any timorous creature for seeking to shun a physical ordeal to which it was unequal." Anther surprises himself in being able to find "a sort of reason, which was not an excuse," for even Royal Langbrith: "Given such a predatory nature as his, was it not in the order of things that there should be another nature formed for his prey? Must not the very helplessness of his victim have been the irresistible lure of his cruelty?" (p. 300). And for James Langbrith, Anther finds "entire excuse." It may be that James instinctively felt what Anther himself had come to feel, that there was "a sort of profanation in the idea" that Mrs. Langbrith should become his wife. Whatever his part has been in causing injury to James Langbrith by keeping the truth about his father from him, Anther now is willing to accept his "share of the retribution as the just penalty of his share in the error" (pp. 301–2).

Not long afterward, Dr. Anther dies of typhoid fever. Interestingly, Hawberk dies just before. Regaining his health and believing that a new life is ahead of him, Hawberk one day slips and falls into icy water at the Langbrith mill. Hawberk's "weakness" having always been "of the body, not of spirit," he dies of pneumonia. But Anther dies of a fever which unsettles his mind, and when he succumbs to the fever at last, he is delirous, "so that it was not known whether his asking for Mrs. Langbrith was or was not from a mind fully master of itself" (p. 317). In the end neither Hawberk nor Anther achieves full reconciliation of mind and body, of spirit and flesh. A perfect wholeness in life is not possible for them.

Returned from Paris and having learned about his father from John Langbrith, James is reconciled with his mother. When she tells her son about Anther's death, James, looking back on the past, is ashamed of the arrogance and folly of his conduct in his "baseless illusion" about his father. Romantically resolving to live a life of renunciation and self-sacrifice, James tells Hope Hawberk that she must give him up. Hope protests that he is being ridiculous, and together they go to Enderby to learn his view of the matter. When James declares that he must make some reparation to Enderby for having asked him to speak at the memorial ceremony, Enderby explains that he had known all along about Royal Langbrith. " 'It seemed to me that no good and much harm could come of revealing the past; that so far as your father was concerned we had no right to enter into judgment, and that so far as God's purposes were concerned we had no right to act upon our conception of what they might be in such a case' " (p. 350). When Enderby is told by James how he learned about his father from John Langbrith,

" 'The rector thought how it was written, "Surely the wrath of man shall praise Thee." It seemed to him that the Divine Providence had not acted inopportunely; and he was contented with the mode in which the young man had learned the worst . . .' " (p. 351).

At the last the question of justice in the case of Royal Langbrith is discussed by Enderby and his wife. Mrs. Enderby, as Edwin Cady has observed, is "possessed of an inherited Puritan conscience," [5] and she feels that Royal Langbrith should have paid for the suffering he caused. Her husband suggests that perhaps Langbrith did suffer in " 'his consciousness in his sudden death that he could not undo the evil he had done.' " Then, in a flight beyond the imaginative reach of his wife, Enderby expresses what Edwin Cady feels is the "highest guess at the riddle of the painful earth Howells could reach after more than twenty years of trying in serious fiction." [6]

> "How do we know but that in that mystical legislation, as to whose application to our conduct we have to make our guesses and inferences, there may not be a law of limitations by which the debts overdue through time are the same as forgiven? No one was the poorer through their non-payment in Royal Langbrith's case; in every high sort each was the richer. It may be the complicity of all mortal being is such that the pain he inflicted was endured to his behoof, and that it has helped him atone for his sins as an acceptable offering in the sort of vicarious atonement which has always been in the world." (p. 369)

However attractive Enderby's appeal to a "mystical legislation" at work in human affairs may be, there remains Dr. Anther's guess at the riddle of painful earth. When Judge Garley had asked Anther whether he believed in the "supernatural," Anther replied:

"'no . . . only in the natural'" (p. 293). Both
views are presented in the novel as hypotheses to account for what happens in the experience of the char
acters. In Howells' realist view both Enderby and
Anther are right in guessing at the ultimate intention
of life from its actualities; but, where absolute knowledge eludes man, he cannot do more than guess—as
best he can. Whatever "law" is operative in the complicity of experience, the guesses about its nature are
various in the novel, and the final meaning of the
truth about Royal Langbrith is left open. If the secret
life of Royal Langbrith is not revealed to the people of
Saxmills, Howells does hint at a reconciliation of the
problem of evil and good in the novel in the union of
James Langbrith and Hope Hawberk. They represent
the continuity of life and keep alive hope for a future
which assimilates the past without being deadened by
it. Pragmatism, said William James, "will entertain
any hypothesis . . . will consider any evidence. . . ,
Her only test of probable truth is what works best in
the way of leading us, what fits every part of life best
and combines with the collectivity of experience's demands, nothing being omitted." [7] Anther's eventual
growth and his acceptance of his situation, and James
Langbrith's broadened perception of his own situation
point their awareness of the complicity in which they
share for whatever good and evil may be theirs. Man's
task, Howells implies, is to live as decently as he can
within the limitations of his knowledge of the truth.

THE LEATHERWOOD GOD is a story about a man and a
community—Leatherwood, Ohio—in the early years
of the nineteenth century. The man, Joseph Dylks,
arrives in Leatherwood, claiming that he is God and
promising to bring there the New Jerusalem. A problem in the novel is to understand the significance of
Joseph Dylks. Closely connected with this problem is
the personal drama of Nancy Gillespie Dylks Billings,
symbolic in the novel of man's divided existence and
of his union in division. A third character of major
importance is Matthew Braile, Leatherwood's "justice
of the peace," as he calls himself. Writing to Hamlin
Garland, Howells said of Braile: "He is a sort of grim
chorus, but he has his part in the action." [1] Dylks,
Nancy, and Braile are the chief figures in the novel,
and their story is of lasting interest.

Dylks appears in Leatherwood at a religious meeting in the "Temple." During a silence which follows
after the preacher has asked the congregation what it
shall pray for, some one calls out for "Salvation!" Abel
Reverdy, who is something of a mental and moral
albino in the novel and whom Oscar Firkins described
as "wedded so absolutely" to his wife,[2] tells Matthew
Braile about the incident at the Temple.

". . . then says he, 'What shall we pray for?' and just
then there came a kind of snort, and a big voice shouted

out, 'Salvation' and then there came another snort,—
'Hooff'—like there was a scared horse got loose right in
there among the people; and some of 'em jumped up
from their seats, and tumbled over the benches, and
some of 'em bounced off, and fell into fits, and the
women screeched and fainted, thick as flies." [3]

The person described as being horselike by Abel
and who shouts for "Salvation" is Joseph Dylks. Dylks
is tall and muscular. What is striking about him, however, is his darkness. He wears a black coat and has "a
suit of long, glossy, jet-black hair." His eyes, Abel says,
are "like two coals, just black fire, kind of." The darkness Abel sees in Dylks suggests the novel's mystery in
the commonplace. Significantly, most of the religious
activity in Leatherwood is at night. Howells makes use
of a Hawthorian symmetry of darkness and light,
though. The story begins with Abel Reverdy's account
to Matthew Braile in early morning and closes with
Braile's account of the Dylks story to T. J. Mandeville
at night.

At the time of Dylks's appearance in Leatherwood,
says the narrator,

> the community had become a center of influence, spirit-
> ual as well as material, after a manner unknown to later
> conditions . . . The population . . . enjoyed an ease
> of circumstance not so great as to tempt them or their
> thoughts from the other world and fix them on this.
> . . . Religion was their chief interest . . . but the gen-
> eral prosperity had so far relaxed the stringency of their
> several creeds that their distinctive public rite had come
> to express a mutual toleration. (pp. 3–4)

With the coming of Dylks, Leatherwood passses from
a state of toleration to one of disruption and discord.
Families are divided and turn on themselves in hatred
and violence. Internecine war ceases in Leatherwood
only when Dylks leaves it and dies. Matthew Braile,

who is directly responsible for Dylks's departure, urges tolerance on the people, and the peaceful order of life is restored in Leatherwood.

Matthew Braile, a deistical freethinker and reader of Tom Paine, stands in the novel for the light of reason as expressed in civil law. If there is the religious Temple in Leatherwood, there is also Braile's house, which he calls the " 'Temple of Justice—Justice of the Peace' " (p. 14). Keen-eyed and sharp-witted, Braile, throughout much of the novel, perches in a chair tilted against his house and remarks on Leatherwood's folly, especially the folly of its conduct as regards Dylks. As the light of reason, Braile seems to find that the best time of day is early morning; and Howells shows him to us as forever smoking a last pipe of tobacco before going into breakfast with his wife. Her part of the house is the kitchen. The other part is Braile's law office. If Braile is generally regarded in Leatherwood as lacking in religious belief, it is made up for by his wife. Abel Reverdy says to Braile, " 'The way I told 'em to look at it was, Mis' Braile was Christian enough for the whole family. Said *you* knowed more law and *she* knowed more gospel than all the rest of Leatherwood put together' " (pp. 14–15). The double log cabin of the Brailes incorporates both moral and civil law and provides a home for husband and wife. Noting Howells' attraction toward a balanced life, Howard M. Munford has written:

> The distinction between the will and the understanding had the further effect of sensitizing Howells to the duality of man's nature which he described variously as the head and the heart, the intellect and the conscience, reason and passion. His Swedenborgian background taught him the necessity of the proper balance of these two elements for an integrated personality and

the proper development of character. . . . The over-development of either, or their separation, is contrary to order.[4]

There is a hint that the domestic situation in the Braile household is not as fruitful as it might be, however. Since the death of their son Jimmy when a boy, the Brailes have been childless.

Nancy Gillespie Dylks Billings, who, Howells told Hamlin Garland, "is the chief figure of the drama," [5] is the wife—though this is not known in Leatherwood—of Joseph Dylks. Dylks had left Nancy some years ago, just after their marriage and just at the time of Joey Dylks's birth. Believing that Dylks must be dead, Nancy marries Laban Billings. With the return of Dylks, Nancy, her brother David tells her, stands convicted of bigamy in the eyes both of the law and of God. At David's insistence and because of the demand of her own conscience, Nancy sends Laban away, though it nearly kills her to do so. Later, she denounces a God who sets such snares for human beings. As the wife of Dylks, who claims he is God, and as the wife of Laban, Nancy would seem to be married in both a supernatural and natural sense. The problem and the mystery in her marriage are the terms of the novel: the relationship between the one and the many, the invisible and the visible, the spirit and the flesh, transcendent law and human law. With Dylks's death, Nancy is free to return to Laban; but the human complicity, essentially mysterious, is continued in Nancy's marriage and is symbolically pointed in Nancy's son, Joey Dylks Billings.

When Jane Gillespie, David's daughter, is irresistibly drawn by a "power" she feels in Dylks, David is outraged but helpless; for, should David attempt to take action against Dylks, the latter threatens to expose Nancy's bigamy. David complains to Nancy that

he cannot understand what has gotten into Jane:
" 'Up to a year ago she was like she had always been, as
biddable as a child, and meek and yielding in every
way. All at once she's got stiff-necked and wilful.' " To
this Nancy replies:

> "She couldn't tell you why, herself, David. We are all
> that way—good little girls—and then all of a sudden
> wilful women. I don't know what changes us. It's
> harder on us than it is on you. It came on me like a
> thief in the night and stole away my sense. It gave
> Joseph Dylks his chance over me; if it had been sooner
> or later I should have known he was a power of dark-
> ness as far as I could see him. But my eyes were holden
> by my self-conceit, and I thought he was an angel of
> light." (p. 85)

In a scene between Nancy and Dylks soon afterward,
she says to him: " 'Oh, I don't say you wasn't handsome; that was what done it for me when I made you
my God; but I won't make you my God now, though
you're as handsome as ever' " (pp. 99–100). The
power that changed Nancy and, later, Jane, we may
call sex. Edwin H. Cady writes: "Howells knew of
course that the path from evangelical excitement in
camp meetings to powerful sexual stimulation was
notoriously short and that the bushes around a revival
full of 'power' were likely to be well inhabited. And he
suggests by every method short of open statement that
the ground of Dylks's *mana* was sexual." [6] Even so,
Howells' novel does not distinguish absolutely between physical and spiritual love. Such a distinction is
made by the characters in their experience, but the
truth of that experience is incomplete. To explain
Jane Gillespie's attraction to Dylks—and Nancy's before that—as merely sexual is to ignore the religious
context of Dylks's power. Whether the power of God
and the power of sex are really one or different is

knowledge of a reality which man does not have, and it is this ambiguity with which the novel deals.

Though Dylks may seem a rank imposter and confidence man, his progress in Leatherwood is nonetheless remarkable. Among his followers he is able to count two of Leatherwood's first citizens, Richard Enraghty, the school master, and Peter Hingston, wealthy miller and farmer. Dylks is able to persuade Enraghty that he is St. Paul and Hingston that he is St. Peter. That which acted to persuade Enraghty and Hingston, however, was not wholly Dylks's power. As Dylks later tells Matthew Braile: " 'You think I had to lie to them, to deceive them, to bewitch them. I didn't have to do anything of the kind. They did the lying and deceiving themselves.' " Just as Nancy had admitted to a kind of "self-conceit" as informing her attraction to Dylks, it is suggested that Enraghty and Hingston have been prompted by a subtle egoism to seek absolute self-realization through their God, Dylks. Whatever power it is that acts in Enraghty and Hingston, it is disciplined in the human economy of the novel by counterbalancing influences of the kind represented in Braile's reason and law, and in his urging of tolerance and respect for familial duty in Leatherwood society. At the last, for instance, though Nancy does not reject belief in God, it is clear that her first thought is for her husband and family. The implication is that Nancy's fulfillment must be in terms of her human actuality.

The trial of Dylks by Matthew Braile is occasioned by Dylks's failure to perform a promised miracle. A "sign" is asked of him by the people, and he promises to turn a bolt of cloth into a "seamless raiment." The miracle is to be worked at night in Hingston's mill; but the "seamless raiment" promised by Dylks becomes instead a tatter of rags when the cloth is torn by a mob of both believers and unbelievers in a wrangle that begins when the actuality of the miracle is disputed. In his portrait of the woman who volunteers the bolt of cloth, Howells brings to a focus the pathos and potential tragedy of life when man is victimized by his own beliefs.

In the August twilight which now began to pale the hot sunset glow, as if she had waited to come alone, in her pride or in her shame, the woman who was bearing the body of the miracle to the place where the wonder was to be wrought came last of all to pass Nancy where she sat at her door. She was that strong believer who in her utter trust, when she heard that cloth would be needed for the seamless raiment of his miracle, had offered to provide it; and now, neither in pride nor in shame, but in defiance of her unbelieving husband, she was bearing away from her house the bolt of linsey-woolsey newly come from the weaver, which was to have been cut into the winter's clothing of her children. She had spun the threads herself and dyed them, and they had become as if they were of her own flesh and blood. She carried the bolt wrapped about with her shawl, bearing it tenderly in her arms, as if it were indeed her flesh and blood, her babe which she was going to lay upon an altar of sacrifice. (p. 116)

Following the mill episode the unbelievers, led by Jim Redfield, hunt down and capture Dylks, who had hidden away in the houses of believers. Held in the Temple for trial next morning by Matthew Braile, Dylks is abused and mocked. One woman, estranged from her husband because she would not believe in Dylks, strikes him on his cheeks. "The guards struggled with her, and a man stooped over Dylks and voided a mouthful of tobacco juice in his face; another lashed him on the head with a switch of leatherwood: all in a squalid travesty of the supreme tragedy of the race. As if a consciousness of the semblance touched the gospel-read actors in the drama, they shrunk from what they had done, and lost themselves in the crowd" (pp. 143–44). Howells' allusion to Christ, his mention of "the gospel-read actors in the drama" of Dylks, and the Biblical character of the names of many of the characters, all point to the universality of his theme.

At the trial next morning, Jim Redfield charges Dylks with professing to be "Almighty God." When Braile asks Dylks whether he is God, Dylks answers: " 'Thou sayest.' " Braile is enraged. He "might have been willing to burlesque the case from his own disbelief, but he could not suffer the desecration of the hallowed words." Unable to find that Dylks has violated any civil law, Braile acquits Dylks. There is, Braile says, no " 'law against a man's being God . . . unless it's some law of the Bible, which isn't in force through reënactment in Ohio' " (pp. 149–50). So Dylks is acquitted, without the trial's proving whether he is or is not God. Dylks himself later says to Braile that " 'if you keep telling them you're Jesus Christ, there's nothing to prove you ain't, and if you tell them you're God, who ever saw God, and who can deny it?' " Braile smiles at this. It strikes him that "it must have been so with all the impostors in the world, from Mahomet up and down" (p. 173).

Matthew Braile, with his faith in the law and in the wisdom of common sense, concludes that Dylks is an imposter. From Mahomet "up and down," the impostors have been deluded by their own vanity, Braile believes. In Braile's deism, God lives far off from the world of men and does not reveal himself in ordinary experience; and in that experience of common life Braile sees no mystery. Interrupting a quarrel between believers and unbelievers after Dylks's trial, Braile commands: " 'Now, you fellows, both sides, go home, and look after your corn and tobacco; and you women, you go and get breakfast for them, and wash up your children and leave the Kingdom of Heaven alone for a while' " (p. 152). We may not say of Braile, as William James did of Emerson, that "he could perceive the full squalor of the individual fact, but he could also see the transfiguration." [7] Edwin H. Cady has observed that Braile's name may mean one "who could read in the dark." [8] The name is ironic, though, when we remember that in the novel Braile is a creature of the morning and sees by the light of reason. But Braile is blinded by his own faith, failing to perceive that ordinary facts may be more than what they seem to him. Howells' realism recognizes that facts in themselves prove nothing. Facts, in William James's words again, "are not *true*." "Truth," James continued, "is the function of the beliefs that start and terminate among" the facts.

Dylks and Braile together stand for a complementary darkness and light in Howells' novel. The formulation suggests a dualism in experience, but in Howells' fiction the light and the dark are interdependent in complicity. Dark and light are, in other words, not fixed. They are emergent, as is reality itself. But while Dylks and Braile serve to establish the issues and problems of the novel, the human conflict arising from them is dramatically centered in Nancy Gillespie, whom Howells called the "chief figure of the drama." Wedded to both Dylks and Laban, Nancy is pledged to two different kinds of life which would exclude each other in law. Her dilemma is that she is committed at once to both sides in a dualistic formulation of existence. A decision by Nancy in favor of Dylks alone would mean, by implication, a decision for existence as essentially one in "power." Sex and God would be One. On one occasion, for example, Dylks urges Nancy to take him back. The two of them together, he declares, " 'could swing the world.' " Together they would make " 'the perfect Godhead, male and female, for the greatest sign of all' " (p. 99). In returning to Laban Billings, however, Nancy does not altogether free herself from Dylks, for he lives on in her son. When Nancy at last tells Joey about his father, she explains to him that his "real" father was Dylks but that his "true" father is Laban. Nancy seems to mean that Dylks was the real father in that he helped give life to Joey. Laban, as the true father, loves and provides for Joey and Nancy, and, thus, makes possible the continuance of the family's life. To choose the true rather than the real father, however, is a choice necessarily imperfect; for, insofar as Dylks shares in some ultimate reality as the "power" of life, all human existence is dependent on that power. Dylks's assertion that the power of life is absolute with him amounts to a denial of the expression of that power in the humbler life of Laban Billings and others like him. In Laban we have a type of Matthew Braile's ordinary man working in love at the daily tasks of ordinary existence. Dylks may be Joey's real father, but Laban is his true one; and in Joey the complicity of the real and the true is the mystery of ordinary life.

"Salvation" in *The Leatherwood God* is not conceived in terms of the righteous self-seeking prompted by the absolutism of Dylks. Rather, it is conceived as a common enterprise in which all men are involved together. The means of salvation are those urged by Matthew Braile on the people of Leatherwood: tolerance, fidelity to one's daily task, and love for one's family, symbol of man's union in difference. But it should be understood that the means urged are possible conditions for the achievement of salvation; and

salvation is incomplete and uncertain. The commonsense light of Matthew Braile is limited in vision in
view of that darkness embodied in Dylks and his story.
In a letter to Henry James—the son of the philosopher
—Howells said that he was reading William James's
book and thanked his son for it. Then, referring to
The Leatherwood God, Howells said the latter would
be at fault if he did not find the moral and meaning of
The Leatherwood God in its commonsense psychol-
ogy.[9] I think we would be mistaken, however, to understand Howells as implying that the common sense
of Matthew Braile represents the author's view in the
novel. Attractive as Braile may be, his is still a limited
view of the truth of experience in the novel. Braile is
given the last words on Dylks. Yet, even as he tells the
Dylks story to T. J. Mandeville, Braile is interrupted
by the night's coming on; and he breaks off in his
story, waiting, he says, to finish it in the morning.
Dylks's story is one of both darkness and light, and
the two meet and mingle in Nancy's life. Her answer
to the mystery, the novel's real commonsense one, is
to go on living as best she can.

SUBTITLED "An Idyl of the Middle Eighteen-Seventies," *The Vacation of the Kelwyns* is a delightful comedy of manners that is quietly satiric about life lived in the strenuous mood. In the book, published in the year of the author's death, 1920, "the aged Howells," says Richard Chase, "makes a virtue out of not trying very hard. . . ." [1] Those in the story who do try very hard to keep intact their tight little world are the vacationing Kelwyns. That theirs is not all the world, and that they can not make it so, is the theme of the novel.

Middle-class people of a New England university town, where Mr. Kelwyn teaches Historical Sociology, the Kelwyns, with their two boys, manage a life of "refined frugality" on the combination of Mr. Kelwyn's salary and what little money Mrs. Kelwyn has of her own. Well-read and scholarly, Kelwyn is highly regarded by his students and is himself inclined to feel that his office is "a very high one, and could not be magnified too much." [2] Kelwyn is supported in the idea of his self-importance by Mrs. Kelwyn, who often wishes that the board of overseers could know the "influence" her husband has with his students. His own father having been a farm boy and country merchant who had wanted his son to have an intellectual career, Kelwyn, since first entering school, has led a life "as purely intellectual as if he had been detached from the soil by generations of culture and affluence." Living largely in the present without any sense of the past or of his ties with it, Kelwyn is content in his family and his work. His friends are nice people. About Mrs. Kelwyn it is perhaps enough to say that her life is centered in her family and that she is "a New England housekeeper of the most exacting sort, with a conscience that gave those she loved very little peace, in its manifold scruples, anxieties, and premonitions" (p. 2).

The time of the story is the centennial summer of 1876, and the Kelwyns are looking for a summer vacation place. In the past they had commonly boarded at a farm or a hotel, but circumstances had never been "in the perfection" Mrs. Kelwyn desired for herself and her family. When the opportunity arises for them to rent a Shaker house in New Hampshire, the Kelwyns believe that their problem is solved. Having come on hard times in its advanced age, the Shaker community, in violation of "the law of its social being," has had increasingly to look to the outside world for stay and support. An arrangement is made between the Shakers and the Kelwyns for the latter to rent an old "Family" house of the Shakers for a year. The Kelwyns will stay in the house for the summer, and the house will be kept for them by a tenant family brought in to work the Shaker land. The Kites, the tenant family, will keep the produce of the land and have the Family house, rent free, for the remainder of the year after the Kelwyns leave. In addition they will receive from the Kelwyns a small fee as board. With all being provided for in their particular needs, the situation seems ideal. In their delight with what they feel will be a "perfect" thing, the Kelwyns conceive themselves as having "complete control of the situation."

> The house would be their house, and the farmer would be their tenant at will. If they did not like him or his wife, if they did not find them capable or faithful, they could turn them out-of-doors any day; and they could not be turned out themselves, or molested, so long as they paid the Shakers the absurd trifle they asked for rent. It seemed impossible that they could fail of their pleasure in such circumstances. (p. 12)

The "perfect arrangement" which the Kelwyns intend their situation to be is strikingly at odds in an America celebrating the centennial of its independence from England. With the Shakers as landlords, the Kelwyns as a sort of effete aristocracy, and the Kites as tenant farmers, the "perfect arrangement" suggests a feudalistic social and economic system more appropriate to old rather than New England. As a spokesman for democracy, said Delmar Gross Cooke, Howells never failed to test "the aristocracy and plutocracy which have taken foothold on our soil by the principles of liberty, equality, and fraternity for which we still profess to stand." [3] In effect, the Kelwyn plan proposes a political hierarchy with the Kelwyns themselves as overlords to the Kites. Howells' novel shows, though, that differences among persons are the result not so much of absolute qualities inhering in individuals as they are the result of the actualities of circumstance and habit, which are themselves accentuated by social conventions. The actual differences between the ignorant and squalid Kites and the refined Kelwyns are, of course, made by themselves; but the "perfect arrangement" of the Kelwyns only serves to heighten the differences between themselves and the Kites and to widen the gap between the two families which, ironically, live in the idealistically selfless

"Family" house of the Shakers. Here, again, Howells hints at the idea of man's division in unity.

The day on which the Kelwyns arrive at their Shaker house is a perfect one of blue sky and fresh, clean air, "as if the spirit of New England housekeeping had entered into Nature, and she had set her house in order for company." The Shaker house is all that Mrs. Kelwyn had imagined it to be, with the exception of its furnishings. She had thought these would be quaint, but she discovers instead a tasteless uniformity about them. They "had no more character than they had in the furniture warerooms where they were bought." The uniformity of the furnishings is nonetheless appropriate to the self-appointed superiority of the Kelwyns, just as it is appropriate to the selfless communal ideal of the Shakers. What had started out as a perfect day turns out to be, when Mrs. Kite serves supper, a small catastrophe. Supper consists of slices of cake, dried apples, English tea — brought by the Kelwyns — that is "strong as lye," butter that is even stronger, an overpowering salt-rising bread, and milk flecked with dirt. Summoning her dignity, Mrs. Kelwyn sends for Mrs. Kite and tells her to bring eggs and hot biscuits. The eggs come limp from the fat of the frying pan, and the biscuits smell of alkali. At the chapter's close, Mrs. Kelwyn wails: " 'What in the world shall we do?' "

Fearing harm from tramps and strong in his sense "of the sacredness of property rights," Kelwyn buys a six-dollar pistol for protection. He soon afterward gives up any idea of using it, however; Mr. Kite, stalwart in strength, will keep off the tramps, Kelwyn reasons. Occasionally the Kites, "unbidden, but unforbidden," join the Kelwyns in after-supper talk on the grass outside the Family house. When Mr. Kite on one of these occasions relaxes and talks of his youth in

Vermont, Kelwyn, fearing himself "in danger of getting on human terms" with Kite, draws back. It surprises the Kelwyns to learn that the Kites "apparently . . . had standing in the neighborhood." Mrs. Kite shows herself as proud of her husband's ability to speak words of French, though he cannot read English. Indeed there is an air of self-respect and pride about the Kites that the Kelwyns, ironically, cannot understand. Mrs. Kite is looked up to with respect and admiration by her husband, her sons, and the Canadian farm hand who lives with them. This is a fact "which in its way became one of Mrs. Kelwyn's trials, and remained for her to the last a baffling anomaly."

Into the "nightmare" which the Kelwyns feel themselves to be living, comes Mrs. Kelwyn's twenty-seven-year-old cousin, Parthenope Brook. Born in Naples—she was named "in recognition of the classic name of the city"—of artistic American parents and herself artistically inclined, Parthenope, or "Thennie" as she is more familiarly called, is a pretty and idealistic young lady from Boston who has decided to visit the Kelwyns for "a fresh point of view" (p. 54). Parthenope has gathered her ideals out of her reading in novels—George Eliot, Charles Reade, Mrs. Gaskell—and out of "the nascent American fictionists of the *Atlantic Monthly* school." These latter inculcate in Parthenope "a varying doctrine of eager conscience, romanticized actuality, painful devotion, and bullied adoration, with auroral gleams of religious sentimentality" (p. 56). "A product not only of foreign education but very distinctly of the highest Emersonian culture," says Richard Chase, Parthenope "is intensely romantic and idealistic." [4] Parthenope's education is continued in Howells' story under the tutelage of Elihu Burritt Emerance, an "empiricist" and jack-of-all trades, who aspires to write for the stage. Parthenope and Emerance make a complementary pair in Howells' study of multiple contrasts and, at the end, they are in love and will marry. Early in the novel the author comments on a complementary balance in the moods of married life in regard to the Kelwyns. "It is one of the advantages of marriage that both the parties to the compact are seldom in the same mind or mood, and one of its disadvantages that with this useful variance they are as often hurtful as helpful to each other. They cannot always agree about a question, though they see both sides of it. If one is cheerful they keep a sort of balance, though the other is gloomy, even though they do not unite in final gayety" (p. 39). We understand that if this is not a "perfect arrangement," it is at least, pragmatically speaking, a working one.

Parthenope and Emerance take pride in their different points of view. Emerance, experimental and empirical, believes that abstractions by which to guide life are to be discovered in experience. For example, he has done some teaching, and it is his opinion that teaching is most successful when it asks those being taught to be imaginatively dramatic. Arithmetic and geography are best learned by imagining situations in which one would use these things. Parthenope, arguing that one must always take into consideration the "ideal," finds Emerance's theory artistically insufficient. Parthenope says that she never acts on "impulse"; that would be "immoral." For all that, however, Parthenope very often acts on impulse, and she enjoys it. It was by impulse that she came to the Kelwyns in the first place; it is by impulse that she gives coffee to a travelling bear-leader's performing bear when it has been stunned by a flash of lightning; and at the end of the novel she can hardly wait to tell her Aunt Julia what a "wild thing" she has done in falling in love with Emerance. The point Howells is making, as Richard Chase has seen, is that there is a place for both impulse and principle in the conduct of life. It is in this sense that Parthenope and Emerance balance each other, she in her insistence on the ideal and he in his experimentalism. Parthenope's complaint about Emerance is that he has no sense of direction or of purpose in life, and something of his many-sided character is perhaps suggested in his being named after Elihu Burritt, "the learned blacksmith" (p. 241). If there is in Emerance an Emersonian quality of independence—he tells Parthenope that what he likes about her is "your self-reliance"—he has lacked any ideal until he finds it in Parthenope. She, on the other hand, dreaming of an ideal hero, falls in love with the empiricist and develops practical attitudes in herself.

Actualities in Howells' novel have little respect for the intentions of the characters. So far as the Kelwyns are concerned, they had intended to be in complete control of their situation, and, if the Kites did not work out, they could be put out; but it is not so easy as the Kelwyns had thought. In the end they are unable to ask the Kites to leave, and it is the Kelwyns themselves who move out. Richard Chase asks whether the Kites, inefficient and ignorant, are "to be treated as criminals or unfortunate victims of their environment . . . . And in the matter of practical action, should the Kelwyns fire the Kites or respond to the moral impulse to try to improve them?" [5] The questions are hard ones and admit of no easy answers, nor does Chase offer any. For that matter, neither does the novel—unless it be at the deeper and more complex level of intricate human relationship. At the end, as the Kelwyns are preparing to leave the Shaker house for their stone cottage, the feelings between them and the Kites are complex. There is a feeling of warmth on both sides; and relief is mixed with regret in the recognition by the families that, after all, they are isolated in their humanity and must, henceforth, live in separate houses. But having given up the rigid situation between them, it is as if the two families are able now to accept each other on their own terms. At the very end, for example, when Kelwyn generously imagines that perhaps he has some private share in the public debt owed to people like the Kites, his wife warns him that if he puts that into his lectures he will lose his influence. Kelwyn laughs—"sadly. 'Then I won't do it. If I can't exert my influence without losing it I won't exert it.' The notion has pleased him, and now he laughed cheerfully" (p. 257). It was at the beginning of the novel, we remember, that Kelwyn's pride in his "influence" over his students was mentioned. Now, at the last he has a sense of humility in his limitations in the face of complex and ambiguous actualities and is able to accept himself in this light. By restraining his influence over others, Kelwyn discovers freedom to live within himself. Letting down in their moral strenuousness, the Kelwyns can live more truly comfortably in the great world than they could in their tight little one. Thus, Howells' whole novel, as Richard Chase observes, "moves away from the taut clash of moral abstractions and self-righteous aggressions to an idyllic celebration of the mere pleasure and contentedness with life, the vital quotidian nourishment the characters find by relaxing into the easier conditions of their being." [6]

Howells invites us to share in his idyl by revealing to us some of the romance of the great world in its colorful diversity. At the edge of the little world of the Kelwyns and of Emerance and Parthenope we catch glimpses of a travelling bear-leader and his performing bear, of a van of gypsies who tell fortunes, of a gigantic Negro skulking through a wood which surely is primeval, and of a troop of Italians from far Genoa. These persons move outside of the restrictions of local customs and conventions and reveal a vitality and freedom that is absent from the lives of the Kelwyns. Even the Kites furnish us a kind of real life romance in their son Arthur and his old and half-blind horse. Mrs. Kelwyn had not wanted her boys to play with Arthur because she feared he would corrupt them. It comes out at the last, however, that Arthur has stolen pies from his mother to give to the bear-leader when he was sick with a cold caught in the rain. Hearing this, Kelwyn jokingly calls Arthur a hero; and almost at once he and Emerance speculate on the moral issues involved in a case where a boy steals from his mother. In a surge of warm feeling, Parthenope stands up for Arthur; and it is a nice touch in the comedy that Howells should have his idealistic young lady supporting the cause of the heroic Arthur. That Arthur here should be a boy who stole pies from his mother to give to a sick man is an instance of a not ignoble adventure in the romance of real life. When Arthur's horse is discovered to be dead at the close of the story, the Kelwyn boys are upset; they had wanted to ride him to their new home. Kelwyn tells them, however, that they " 'can't ride him if he's dead and you want to go anywhere' " (p. 254).

Howells' last novel, written when he was eighty-three, is remarkably young in spirit. There is about the story, wrote Oscar Firkins, "a certain salubrity in the moral atmosphere to which nothing you might care to shut out is quite so unlovable as expulsions and exclusions." [7] For in his last novel, Howells, as before, opens the door to life. Indeed, all his art as a pragmatic realist was to keep life open in his fiction. What the Kelwyns glimpse when they let themselves go is that great world which, Howells knew, always awaits our discovery.

HAVING SAID in my introduction that Howells, in his literary realism, and William James, in his pragmatism, shared in common a basic attitude toward life, I would like to try now to formulate that attitude. It can best be described, I think, by saying that both Howells and James conceived man as living in an open world, a world which is yet unfinished in its meaning and in which man himself is the maker of that meaning. Belonging to this attitude is the affirmation by both Howells and James that man is not helplessly passive before the world, but, rather, that he acts upon it and in so acting creates it. Literally and figuratively, man is the actor; and the world he makes as he goes along is the great drama he enacts. For both Howells and James there was give and take between the world out there and man in himself. There was significant interplay between object and subject. Man made the world out there, but what he made of it he at the same time made of himself. Howells called this situation "complicity." Involved in it is the matter, central to Howells' fiction, of point of view. Like James, Howells knew that what a person did make of the world was intimately related to the way he looked at it. In the realist's terms, this was the person's "slice of life," his sense of reality. Yet, no view caught all there was to reality. It was always something more than any of its definitions, and it was in this possibility of reality's always being something more than it seemed to be that Howells found his vision of the romance of the commonplace.

1 — A Foregone Conclusion

1. William Dean Howells, *A Foregone Conclusion* (Edinburgh, David Douglas, 1905), p. 7. Subsequent citations are parenthetical in the text and refer to this edition. First published: Boston: James R. Osgood and Company, 1875.

2. Olov W. Fryckstedt, *In Quest of America: A Study of Howells' Early Development as a Novelist* (Upsala, Harvard University Press, 1958), p. 152.

3. *Ibid.*, p. 153.

4. Delmar Gross Cooke, *William Dean Howells, A Critical Study* (New York: E. P. Dutton & Company, 1922), pp. 174–75.

5. George N. Bennett, *William Dean Howells: The Development of a Novelist* (Norman: University of Oklahoma Press, 1959), p. 58.

6. Edwin H. Cady, *The Road to Realism: The Early Years, 1837–1885, of William Dean Howells* (Syracuse: Syracuse University Press, 1956), p. 190.

7. William James, *Pragmatism and Four Essays from "The Meaning of Truth"* (New York: Meridian Books, Inc., 1955), p. 47.

8. Henry James, "Howells' 'Foregone Conclusion,'" *The Nation*, XX (Jan. 7, 1875), 12.

9. *Life in Letters of William Dean Howells*, ed. Mildred Howells (New York: Doubleday, Doran & Company, Inc., 1928), I, 198.

10. Bennett, p. 58.

11. *Life in Letters*, I, 198.

2 – The Lady of the Aroostook

1. William Dean Howells, *The Lady of the Aroostock* (Boston: Houghton, Mifflin and Company, 1888), p. 3. Subsequent citations are parenthetical in the text and refer to this edition. First published: Boston: Houghton, Osgood and Company, 1879.

2. George N. Bennett, *William Dean Howells, The Development of a Novelist* (Norman: University of Oklahoma Press, 1959), p. 71.

3. Olov W. Fryckstedt, *In Quest of America: A Study of Howells' Early Development as a Novelist* (Upsala, Harvard University Press, 1958), p. 156.

4. William Wasserstrom, "William Dean Howells: The Indelible Stain," *New England Quarterly*, XXXII (December, 1959), 487.

5. Edwin H. Cady, *The Road to Realism: The Early Years, 1837–1885, of William Dean Howells* (Syracuse: Syracuse University Press, 1956), p. 186.

3 – The Undiscovered Country

1. Olov W. Fryckstedt, *In Quest of America: A Study of Howells' Early Development as a Novelist* (Upsala, Harvard University Press, 1958), p. 187.

2. George N. Bennett, *William Dean Howells: The Development of a Novelist* (Norman: University of Oklahoma Press, 1959), p. 100.

3. William Dean Howells, *The Undiscovered Country* (Boston: Houghton, Mifflin and Company, 1890), p. 419. Subsequent citations are parenthetical in the text and refer to this edition. First published: Boston: Houghton, Mifflin and Company, 1880.

4. Fryckstedt, p. 188.

5. Oscar Firkins, *William Dean Howells, A Study* (Cambridge: Harvard University Press, 1924), p. 92.

4 A Modern Instance

1. Edwin H. Cady, *The Road To Realism* (Syracuse: Syracuse University Press, 1956), p. 212.

2. William Dean Howells, *A Modern Instance*, ed. William M. Gibson (Riverside Editions; Boston: Houghton Mifflin and Company, 1957), p. 288. Subsequent citations of the novel are parenthetical in the text and refer to this edition. In view of Howells' early interest in Emanuel Swedenborg, it may be that in exploring the motive-deed issue in *A Modern Instance* Howells was testing the ethic of Swedenborg. Cf., for example, Emanuel Swedenborg, *Conjugial Love* (New York: American Swedenborg Printing and Publishing Society, 1909), pp. 382–83.

3. Oliver Wendell Holmes, *The Common Law* (Boston: Little, Brown, and Company, 1938), p. 1. First published: Boston: Little, Brown and Company, 1881.

5—The Rise of Silas Lapham

1. William Dean Howells, *The Rise of Silas Lapham*, ed. George Arms (New York: Rinehart and Company, Inc., 1959), p. xv. Subsequent citations are parenthetical in the text and refer to this edition. First published: Boston: Ticknor and Company, 1885.

2. George N. Bennett, *William Dean Howells: The Development of a Novelist* (Norman: University of Oklahoma Press, 1959), p. 152.

3. *William Dean Howells, A Modern Instance*, ed. William M. Gibson (Boston: Houghton Mifflin Company, 1957), p. 158.

4. William Dean Howells, *The Rise of Silas Lapham*, ed. Edwin H. Cady (Boston: Houghton Mifflin Company, 1957), p. xv.

5. Donald Pizer, "The Ethical Unity of *The Rise of Silas Lapham*," *American Literature*, XXXII (November, 1960), p. 323.

6. See Ralph Barton Perry's discussion of the "principle of inclusiveness" in his *In the Spirit of William James* (Bloomington: Indiana University Press, 1958), pp. 132–33, and *passim*.

7. William Dean Howells, *The Rise of Silas Lapham*, ed. Everett Carter (New York: Harper & Brothers, 1958), p. ix.

8. Pizer, p. 325.

9. William James, *Pragmatism and Four Essays from "The Meaning of Truth"* (New York: Meridian Books, Inc., 1955), p. 49.

6 – Annie Kilburn

1. Oscar W. Firkins, *William Dean Howells, A Study* (Cambridge: Harvard University Press, 1924), p. 140.

2. William Dean Howells, *Annie Kilburn* (New York: Harper & Brothers, 1889), p. 47. Subsequent citations are parenthetical in the text and refer to this edition.

3. Edwin H. Cady, *The Realist At War: The Mature Years, 1885–1920, of William Dean Howells* (Syracuse: Syracuse University Press, 1958), p. 82.

4. *Ibid.*

5. *The Rise of Silas Lapham*, ed. George Arms (New York: Rinehart & Company, Inc., 1959), p. 389.

7 – A Hazard of New Fortunes

1. William Dean Howells, *A Hazard of New Fortunes*, Author's Preface, ed. George Arms (New York: E. P. Dutton and Company, Inc., 1952), p. xxi. Subsequent citations of the novel are parenthetical in the text and refer to this edition. First published: New York: Harper and Brothers, 1890.

2. George Arms, Introduction to *A Hazard of New Fortunes*; Everett Carter, *Howells and the Age of Realism*

(Philadelphia: J. B. Lippincott Company, 1954), pp. 201–24; George N. Bennett, *William Dean Howells: The Development of a Novelist* (Norman: University of Oklahoma Press, 1959), pp. 189–99; Edwin H. Cady, *The Realist at War: The Mature Years, 1885–1920, of William Dean Howells* (Syracuse: Syracuse University Press, 1958), pp. 100–113.

3. Carter, pp. 220–22.

4. William James, *Essays in Radical Empiricism* (New York: Longmans, Green and Co. 1912), p. 93.

5. Cf. Ch. 5, "*The Rise of Silas Lapham.*"

6. *A Hazard of New Fortunes*, p. xvii.

8–The Quality of Mercy

1. Edwin H. Cady, *The Realist at War: The Mature Years, 1885–1920, of William Dean Howells* (Syracuse: Syracuse University Press, 1958), p. 164.

2. *Ibid.*, p. 166.

3. William Dean Howells, *The Quality of Mercy* (New York: Harper & Brothers, 1892), p. 20, Subsequent citations are parenthetical in the text and refer to this edition.

4. *The Realist at War*, p. 170; Arnold B. Fox, "Howells' Doctrine of Complicity," *Modern Language Quarterly*, XIII (March, 1952), pp. 56–60.

5. *The Realist at War*, p. 171.

6. William James, *Pragmatism and Four Essays from "The Meaning of Truth"* (New York: Meridian Books, Inc., 1955), p. 105.

7. *Ibid.*

9–The Landlord at Lion's Head

1. William Dean Howells, *The Landlord at Lion's Head* (Library Edition; New York: Harper & Brothers Publishers, 1911), p. 3. Subsequent citations are parenthetical in the text and refer to this edition.

2. Edwin H. Cady, *The Realist at War: The Mature*

Years, 1885–1920, of William Dean Howells (Syracuse: Syracuse University Press, 1958), p. 227.

3. George N. Bennett, *William Dean Howells: The Development of a Novelist* (Norman: University of Oklahoma Press, 1959), p. 207.

4. Unpublished letter, dated July 1, 1897. The letter, a copy of which was furnished to me by George Arms is in the Howells letter file of George Arms, William M. Gibson, and Frederic C. Marston, Jr. The letters are in the possession of George Arms, University of New Mexico, Albuquerque, New Mexico.

5. William James, *Pragmatism and Four Essays from "The Meaning of Truth"* (New York: Meridian Books, Inc., 1955), p. 51.

6. Oscar W. Firkins, *William Dean Howells: A Study* (Cambridge: Harvard University Press, 1924), p. 184.

10 — The Son of Royal Langbrith

1. George N. Bennett, *William Dean Howells: The Development of a Novelist* (Norman: University of Oklahoma Press, 1959), p. 209.

2. William Dean Howells, *The Son of Royal Langbrith* (New York: Harper & Brothers Publishers, 1904), p. 16. Subsequent citations are parenthetical in the text and refer to this edition.

3. Edwin H. Cady, *The Realist at War: The Mature Years, 1885–1920, of William Dean Howells* (Syracuse: Syracuse University Press, 1958), p. 246.

4. *Ibid.*, p. 242.

5. *Ibid.*, p. 248.

6. *Ibid.*, p. 249.

7. William James, *Pragmatism and Four Essays from "The Meaning of Truth"* (New York: Meridian Books, Inc., 1955), p. 61.

11 — The Leatherwood God

1. William Dean Howells, *Life in Letters* (New York: Doubleday, Doran & Company, Inc., 1928), II, p. 356.

2. Oscar W. Firkins, *William Dean Howells: A Study* (Cambridge: Harvard University Press, 1924), p. 204.

3. William Dean Howells, *The Leatherwood God* (New York: The Century Co., 1916), p. 9. Subsequent citations of the novel are parenthetical in the text and refer to this edition.

4. Howard M. Munford, "The Genesis and Early Development of the Basic Attitudes of William Dean Howells." (unpublished Ph. D. dissertation. Harvard, 1950), p. 168.

5. *Life in Letters*, II. p. 356.

6. Edwin H. Cady, *The Realist at War: The Mature Years, 1885–1920, of William Dean Howells* (Syracuse: Syracuse University Press, 1958), p. 267.

7. William James, *Memories and Studies* (New York: Longmans, Green, and Co., 1911), p. 32.

8. Cady, *The Realist at War*, p. 266.

9. Extract from a letter dated August 15, 1913. George Arms, whom I thank for the extract, thinks it likely that the book Howells was reading may have been *Memories and Studies*, which the philosopher's son edited in 1911. The letter is in the Howells letter file of George Arms, William M. Gibson, and Frederic C. Marston, Jr. The letters are in the possession of George Arms, University of New Mexico, Albuquerque, New Mexico.

12 — The Vacation of the Kelwyns

1. Richard Chase, *The American Novel and its Tradition* (New York: Doubleday & Company, Inc., 1957), p. 177.

2. William Dean Howells, *The Vacation of the Kelwyns* (New York: Harper & Brothers Publishers, 1920), p. 4. Subsequent citations are parenthetical in the text and refer to this edition.

3. Delmar Gross Cooke, *William Dean Howells, A Critical Study* (New York: E. P. Dutton & Company, 1922), p. 218.

4. Chase, p. 179.

5. *Ibid.*

6. *Ibid.*, p. 180.

7. Oscar W. Firkins, *William Dean Howells: A Study* (Cambridge: Harvard University Press, 1924), p. 206.